Children in the Assembly
of the Church

*Edited by Eleanor Bernstein, CSJ, and
John Brooks-Leonard*

Liturgy Training Publications

Acknowledgments

It is a very long mile from the original manuscript to a published collection of papers. After authors have done the scholarly work of research and creative composition, manuscripts are prepared for publication. The editors are grateful to Lorraine Strope for thousands of words fed into the computer, to Johan van Parys for assistance in checking footnotes and to Gabe Huck at Liturgy Training Publications for his wise counsel.

This book was prepared at LTP by Elizabeth Hoffman, Jerry Reedy, Sarah Huck, Kari Nicholls and Jill Smith. It was typeset in Minion and Gill Sans and was printed by Award Printing Corporation. The cover photo was taken by Jean Clough.

Library of Congress Cataloging-in-Publication Data

Children in the assembly of the church / edited by Eleanor Bernstein and John Brooks-Leonard.
      p. 99 cm.
    Includes bibliographical references.
    ISBN 0−929650−66−2 (pbk.) : $8.95
      1. Children in public worship—Catholic Church—Congresses.
2. Children's liturgies—Congresses. 3. Worship (Religious education)—Congresses. 4. Catholic Church—Liturgy—Congresses. I. Bernstein, Eleanor. II. Brooks-Leonard, John, 1955−
BX1970.2.C47 1992
264'.02'0083—dc20
92−36339
CIP

To the memory of Mark Searle,
Teacher, Mentor, Friend
† 16 August 1992

Contents

Introduction: Children of the Promise 1
John Brooks-Leonard

Landscaping the Religious Imagination 10
Paul Philibert

Children in the Assembly of the Church 30
Mark Searle

Adults and Children in the Art of Celebration 51
Gertrud Mueller Nelson

Separate Liturgies of the Word with Children? 65
Linda Gaupin

Unpacking the Directory for Masses with Children 81
Joan Patano Vos

Editors and Contributors 100

John Brooks-Leonard

Introduction:

Children of the Promise

Each one of you is a child of God because of your faith in Christ Jesus. All of you who have been baptized into Christ have clothed yourselves with him. There does not exist among you Jew or Greek, slave or free, male or female. All are one in Christ Jesus. Furthermore, if you belong to Christ you are descendants of Abraham, which means you inherit all that was promised. . . . All of you, like Isaac, are children of the promise.[1]

All who belong to Christ are children of the promise. All the baptized without exception have a place in the assembly of God's holy ones. There are no "categories" of belonging to Christ—Jew/Greek, male/female, slave/free, children/adults, teens/aged. We are church because we have been called together, claimed by Christ, immersed into the mystery of his life-giving cross and resurrection for the salvation of the world. Any distinctions within the liturgical assembly or the church ought to be simply expressions and orderings of the great variety of gifts given for the building up of the body of Christ. Each of us—regardless of age or wisdom—is graced to continue this work "till we become one in faith and in the knowledge of the Son of God and become fully mature with the fulness of Christ himself."[2]

Children in the Assembly

No one can deny that the spirit of childhood—singled out by Christ as an essential condition for entering the kingdom of God—is a gift best communicated to us by children themselves. Unfortunately, ecclesial practice for the last several centuries has treated children—even those baptized as infants—as pre-liturgical persons;[3] they are excluded from full sacramental participation "until the age of reason," and in more recent times, marched out of the assembly for separate "liturgies of the word." Society, in general, values children only in so far as they will someday become adults, obtain gainful employment and contribute to the economy. For these and many other reasons, children are increasingly and systematically separated from the adult community to the detriment of all.

The presence of children in the midst of the liturgical assembly, as Mark Searle demonstrates in "Children in the Assembly of the Church," can make a strong statement in the face of such exclusion and neglect. Their presence proclaims and reinforces several Christian convictions concerning the particular gift that children manifest for the building up of the church:

- A child's experience of humanness is complete and whole in itself. A child's value is intrinsic, real in itself. It is false to assume that the value of children is determined by their condition as "potential adults."

- Childhood, like all other authentically human experiences, is a transcendental reality. It thus remains eternally valid and eternally present in the life of every human being.

- Children are a sacrament of the "radical openness to the future" that characterizes Christian faith and conversion. In children we Christians acknowledge both the origins of life and the future of life; in them, we affirm both the power of the human past and the pull toward a human future in the presence of God.

- "Children are parables of God's way of working in the world not because they are docile, innocent, sweet and submissive . . . but because they reveal among us the playfulness and the vulnerability of God. . . . Perhaps that is why we react to children the way we react to parables: with mingled frustration and admiration, annoyance and delight, shock and wonderment."[4]

▪ Children belong to the assembly "not because they will one day grow up and be like us, but because they force us—like parables—to confront the unexpected, to deal with a God who chooses to behave in an un-Godlike manner."[5]

▪ By their presence and by their manner of participation, children are a gift to the whole worshiping community, evidence that worship together is essential for the life of the whole church, "young men and maidens, the old together with children."[6]

▪ In Jesus, God's unique child, we acknowledge one whose divinity is most manifest in weakness, vulnerability, incomprehensible suffering and powerlessness.[7]

▪ The child's native ability to greet the world with an enthusiasm of love and joy, to become so thoroughly taken up with the simplest things—flowers, bugs, raindrops, music boxes—reveals the natural human capacity for contemplation. "The body, mind and emotions are caught up in one all-consuming effort to the exclusion of all other interests to produce the answer or find the way."[8]

Thus, in "Separate Liturgies of the Word with Children?" Linda Gaupin is right to raise some serious questions about the growing practice of providing separate "children's services" as alternatives to their joining the Sunday assembly. If a community is Christian, it is by its very nature inclusive—or is striving to be so. Clericalism (whether by priests, committees or interest groups) and exclusionism (of the poor or rich, young or old, learned or simple, Democrats or Republicans, strong or weak in faith) are antithetical to the liturgy and the surest routes to its demise. Any experience that divorces a child from the reality of the Christian assembly is a misfortune. That reality is *the messy, glorious, sinful and holy church, adults and children called together and gifted by God, empowered by the Spirit to give themselves to explicit communal worship of God.*

At some level of their consciousness, children perceive that "separate but equal" liturgies of the word and/or sacrament marginalize rather than welcome them as an intrinsic part of the faith community. Unfortunately, many of these "children's liturgies" resemble a classroom experience more than liturgy and prayer. Children are apparently considered by some to be incapable of liturgical prayer or of expressing their faith in the rituals of their elders and ancestors.

What about the Directory for Masses with Children?

Many who advocate separate liturgies of the word claim that they are simply implementing the *Directory for Masses with Children*. A careful reading of the document, as Linda Gaupin insists, reveals that the norm is a liturgy where children are present with parents and other family members. The second paragraph of article 17 does permit separate word liturgies for children—but only sometimes and not as a routine or weekly event.

Before rushing to implement article 17, paragraph 2, parish leaders should ask themselves the questions implied in paragraph 1: Have we taken "great care" that the children present at the parish's Sunday and holy day liturgies "do not feel neglected"? Have we taken "great care" to provide children with concrete, sensory ways to increase their ability to participate? When was the last time we began with the sprinkling rite? Had a gospel procession? Sang the responsorial psalm? Used incense? Have we taken "great care" to see that children can hear—even if they cannot fully understand what is being proclaimed in the celebration? Have we taken "great care" to ensure that some account is taken of the children's presence? Have we permitted children to use their gifts (i.e., their talents and training) for music or serving or bearing candles or gifts, etc., alongside the other gifted members of the community? Have we taken "great care" to speak directly to the children in the brief introductory comments and at some point in the homily? If the answer to these questions is "yes," then why would we need "special" separate liturgies of the word for children? Perhaps it is easier to remove children from the Sunday assembly than to deal effectively with what is boring, uninspiring, sloppy and overly cerebral for adults as well as children.[9]

J o h n   B r o o k s - L e o n a r d

Cognitive versus Intuitive/Affective/Experiential

The perceived need for separate liturgies is an indictment of the poor preparation of presiders and other liturgical ministers and of the liturgical mentality that has dominated much of the Western church's prayer for several centuries.[10] The emphasis on the rational and cognitive aspects of the person (the "age of reason" issue is just one example) has left little room for the affective and intuitive facets, which children manifest at an early age. This is obvious in both the triumph of verbalism over other features of liturgical celebration and sacramental minimalism. Our liturgies frequently are wall-to-wall explanations, exhortations, commentaries, words; silence is abhorred, fragrance is forgotten, real bread is rarely broken, gestures are half-hearted, movements are unrehearsed, everything is hurried.

Liturgy is something to be done, not something to be read. When done well, the liturgy takes all that is human and shows it to be a revelation of the divine. More than texts, liturgy includes the silence, gestures, postures, movements, aromas, tastes, visual images, objects, and the entire complex that is our liturgical inheritance. Children can and *do* participate in the many nonverbal elements of the liturgy long before they have mastered verbal language—just watch them "play church." But if the nonverbals are ignored, poorly prepared, sloppily executed and meaningless for ministers and adults alike, it is no wonder that the children feel neglected along with the rest of the assembly!

As Louis Weil has pointed out, children in the assembly are powerful reminders that there is more to being human than rationality. The authentic inclusion of them in parish liturgies will only improve the liturgical experience for adults. The Christian liturgy that is home to children and adults will not let us forget that we have bodies, that we are physical persons, and that our worship (and our Christian life!) involves us with each other—and not merely in perfectly ordered, cerebral ways.[11] Such worship does not require the invention of new forms of bodily involvement as much as immersing ourselves in the postures, gestures and movements of prayer that are already part of our ritual behavior. When the ministers and participants are "caught up" by the presence of God who reveals Self through sacramental signs (i.e., through the verbals and nonverbals together), their actions are inevitably grace-filled; their "play" with and before God is marked by dignity, reverence, beauty, holiness and deep joy.[12]

The *experience* of liturgy is far more significant than catechetical efforts to explain or teach about the liturgy. Children are not to be excluded because they do not understand. For some children and adults with disabilities, what we traditionally label "rational understanding" never develops, and yet they know the presence of "the holy." Those with developmental disabilities are admitted to the sacraments when they manifest "moments of reverence" such as bowing the head when hearing the words of a familiar prayer, clapping hands when hearing a familiar hymn, getting quiet or smiling "knowingly" at the sight of a crucifix or an icon, or when a candle is lighted. Such attitudes form part of the basic, common repertoire of *doing* the liturgy regardless of the participant's age, wisdom or strength. Children and catechumens *participate* first—they *experience*—and later may develop a rational understanding.

As for Masses with children in which only a few adults participate,[13] "it is always necessary to keep in mind that through these eucharistic celebrations children must be led toward the celebration of Mass with adults, especially the Masses in which the Christian community comes together on Sundays."[14] Permitting children to exercise various ministries, the use of singing and music, gestures and actions, visual elements and silence—all reinforce what has been said above concerning the importance of the nonverbal elements of the liturgy. "Dignity, clarity, and simplicity" in gesture and movement along with "liturgical texts spoken intelligibly, unhurriedly, with the necessary pauses" are precisely the aims of every liturgical celebration. The elements, skills, style and gracefulness of Masses with children on school days or similar occasions are the same as those of the Sunday assembly.

Liturgy, Life and Catechesis

A Chinese proverb on the portal of the Children's Museum in Washington, D.C., reads as follows:

John Brooks-Leonard

I hear and I forget.
I see and I remember.
I do and I understand.

Children and adults learn best by doing. How can I understand "for-giveness" if I have never forgiven or been forgiven; if I have never said, "I'm sorry," and been assured with tears and a hug, "That's all right, I for-give you"?

If children are allowed to experience the liturgy over and over again, they imbibe its meanings at the most basic (nonverbal) human level. At that deep level, the intimate and essential connections between liturgy and life are experienced. The human actions that children perform in day-to-day life as members of a family—greeting, embracing, gathering with the family, listening to a good story, asking forgiveness, saying "thank you," washing, eating, celebrating—are essential to the experience of the liturgy. Unfortun-ately, these direct parallels between life and liturgy frequently are suffocated by artificial, spiritless and otherwise impoverished movements and gestures at the liturgy. The liturgical experience of children is formative for them. If the underlying human gestures of the liturgy are minimalized through excessive formalization or excessive casualness, the child will learn (in the formative sense) that Christian faith and its expression in ritual are alien to human life, that they are separate religious categories not directly related to the fabric of day-to-day living.[15]

At the same time, the best liturgical celebration on a Sunday morning cannot alone convey to children the meaning of the Christian life and prayer. That must be learned at home, as Gertrud Mueller Nelson demon-strates in "Adults and Children in the Art of Celebration." The greatest obstacle to a full vision of the meaning of Christian life is the mispercep-tion—even on the part of practicing Christians—that corporate and private prayer are something apart from real life. Regular family prayer is rare and for the most part experienced as artificial. So long as prayer is absent from the home seven days each week, there is little hope that Sunday worship can be other than a foreign intrusion, a routine with little meaning in life. So long as the seasons of the liturgical year lend no "seasoning" to the family table, the cycle of feasts and fasts may as well be disposed of in favor of an interminable "ordinary" time.

Catechists know their work relies heavily on the experiences students have of church and home. As the catechesis of children is transformed from the "teaching information" model to the "mystagogia" model, modern mystagogues will "lead children into the mystery" by helping them unpack the multilayered ramifications of their experiences of liturgy and life and the intimate connection between the two. To use the phrase of Paul Philibert, the rituals and stories of the Christian tradition "landscape children's imaginations" with figures and events that inspire a life patterned on the gospel and shed light on their own spiritual journeys. Liturgical celebrations become once again the ritual expression of our whole life in Christ, and not didactic exercises.

Mission of the Assembly

What is at stake in the matter of "children's liturgies" is not simply good catechetical method or proper liturgical formation, but the integrity of the Christian assembly itself. For it is the assembly's primary mission to witness to the full breadth and length of God's gifts to humankind—in the young and the old, the married and the single, the hale and the sick, the joyful and the bereaved, the robust and the weak. It would be ironic indeed if, at this period in our history when we are striving for greater inclusivity in liturgical language and ministerial praxis, we were to exclude those little ones whom Jesus drew to himself and blessed. We could end up with nothing to pass on to the next generations; we could forfeit our own inheritance as children of the promise.

Notes

The papers in this collection were delivered at *Children of Promise: A Place in the Assembly,* the Twentieth Annual Conference of the Notre Dame Center for Pastoral Liturgy, June 17– 20, 1991. In its original form, this introduction served as the background statement that was given to the speakers before they prepared their presentations; it appeared in a slightly different form in *Assembly* 17:4 (June 1991), 524–526.

[1] Galatians 3:26–29; 4:28.

[2] Ephesians 4:13.

[3] Louis Weil, "Children and Worship," in *The Sacred Play of Children*, edited by Diane Apostolos-Cappadona (New York: Seabury, 1983), 55–59.

[4] Nathan Mitchell, "The Parable of Childhood," *Liturgy* 1:3 (June 1981), 12.

[5] Mitchell, 12.

[6] Psalm 148:12.

[7] Mitchell, 14.

[8] Constance Tarasar, "Taste and See: Orthodox Children at Worship," in *The Sacred Play of Children*, 50. Note the references to the need for contemplation in the *Directory for Masses with Children*, nos. 22, 37, 46 and 48.

[9] See Craig B. McKee, "Mainstreaming vs. Special Education: Do We Really Want Separate Children's Word Liturgies?" Children's Holistic Institute for Liturgical Development, 1990.

[10] Weil, 56.

[11] Weil, 57.

[12] See Xavier John Seubert, "Ritual Embodiment: Embellishment or Epiphany?" *Worship* 63:5 (September 1989), 402–416; and "Weaving a Pattern of Access: The Essence of Ritual," *Worship* 63:6 (November 1989), 490–503.

[13] This is the focus of Chapter III of the *Directory for Masses with Children*, which is explored more fully in the article in this volume by Joan Patano Vos, "Unpacking the Directory for Masses with Children."

[14] *Directory for Masses with Children*, no. 21.

[15] Weil, 59.

Paul Philibert

Landscaping
the Religious Imagination

We live in a funny moment. We imagine ourselves to inhabit the most privileged age of human history. We have an unparalleled capacity to turn natural reality into instruments that serve us. We have mobility, shelter, a variety of comforts and continuous amusement—more than ancient emperors and kings. And though we come from vastly different cultural roots, we now have a common source of moral wisdom, the media, and a common means of communication, television, to unify us into a single culture.

But I call this a "funny" moment. Despite this embarrassment of riches, we live in crisis. The media mete out to us a wisdom that represents the least common denominator in the shared culture bank of our religious and traditional origins. We are on the far end of a decade of unbridled hedonism, unsure of where we are, where we are going, or even where we want to go. Many persons wait passively to be told what will be the emerging theme of human significance in the next age—the new fad.

It is hard to be sure what is wrong, yet the following may prove illuminating. The television industry asks advertisers to pay hundreds of thousands of dollars for 30 seconds of air time. They boast about their share of the market and promise the payoff of audience response. They clearly believe that TV ads are powerful enough to change public reactions toward everything from soda pop to politicians. Yet for more than 20 years the same industry has emphatically denied that its broadcast of a staple diet of murder, crass manipulation, sexual violence against women and the systematic mockery of religious and traditional values is responsible for or related to the astronomical escalation of murders, illegitimate births and violent crimes in our society.[1] This illogical posture of the television industry can be accepted only by those who have become completely numbed by whatever the media purveys to us.

In this funny moment, then, there is bad news, but also good news. The bad news is easy enough to see. Everywhere in the popular culture we find traditional moral values and traditional standards of beauty being ridiculed. Film critic Michael Medved wrote recently: "In the visual arts, in literature, in film, in music of both the popular and classical variety, ugliness has been enshrined as the new standard, as we accept the ability to shock as a replacement for the old ability to inspire."[2]

But the good news is there as well. We are—all of us—"children of promise." St. Paul's original use of that phrase in Romans 8:9 was generated in a context of confrontation and challenge. The Jewish community disowned the Jesus movement; the Roman world criminalized it. Yet Paul still affirmed that Jesus had triumphed over both the law of the Jews and the culture of the Roman empire. For him, the "children of promise" were those who inherit and commit themselves to live the mystery of the Christ despite the obstacles of the surrounding world. In order to empower the early Christian community, he constructed for them a symbolic world that became the controlling factor in their lives of hope.

Paul landscaped their religious imagination with powerful symbols that have become normative for all succeeding generations in the church. He explained that Christ is the firstborn of many brothers and sisters, that Christ's life with them is so intimate as to constitute a single "body," that their identification with Christ is so powerful that Christ lives in them and works in and through them. The combination of their faith and Jesus' gift of his own Spirit achieves this transformation. So radical indeed is the transformation wrought by faith and the Spirit, that Paul describes it as a new creation—a different world from the one of Jewish law and Roman imperial culture. St. Paul's interpretation of Christian life requires believers to live more in a world of symbols than in a world of surrounding objects.

The Zone of Imagination

In what follows, I wish to give the phrase "children of promise," another emphasis. We speak of the children in our families and parishes as the fruit of God's promise to dwell among us and touch our world. Too often we have treated children as inadequate miniature adults whose only fault is that they have not grown large enough and reasonable enough to do exactly what we do. We can see, however, as we look at our cultural predicament, that characteristically we adults turn Paul's challenge of a new creation into mere words rather than an entryway into a symbolic world that heals, sanctifies and empowers. In order to sustain Paul's challenge rather than collapse it, I will probe some of the dynamics that make it possible to dwell as a permanent resident in the world of faith. As we make our way, we will see that our children are promised a privileged role among us—that they are the ones who dwell closest to the original source of life in hope and trust. It is from that world that God's grace reaches us and transforms us through Christian word and sacrament.

Formative Imagination

Our lives are shaped by the images that become the repertory of symbols from which we draw ideas and words. This level of human reality is sometimes referred to as the "deep structure" of our world's meaning, or as the "subtext" of discourse, or as the realm of imagery. In the absence of important objects, each of us has the capacity to create subjective experiences (images) that represent those objects and invest them with meaning, feelings and purpose. Such images are not just imitations of sensory impressions; they include also reconstructions, reinterpretations and fragments of history, as well as symbols that stand for objects and for the way we feel about them.[3] Our images are deeply connected with emotions, either as responses, as expressions or as evocations of feelings. Likewise they are strongly shaped by our attitudes toward our bodies—toward our feelings of beauty, strength, vulnerability and relatedness. Thus, images are the "crossroads" of consciousness: a place where many psychic forces interact and become intertwined with one another.[4]

We humans are deeply rooted in images and symbols because, from the earliest moments of our lives, we are forced to transcend the paralyzing dependency on absorption or fusion with the objects of our desires. The infant begins life without an image or symbol for mother, because during the months in the womb the infant's consciousness was of unity. It is separation that prompts the formation of the concept of "mother," and in the creation of that concept, the infant also creates the experience of nostalgia for the former experience of maternal unity.

As infants, we create our world of other objects by the same ironic structure: The concept or mental image of a thing comes to be established within us precisely at the point that we realize that it has been taken away from us.[5] Although formal education in the classroom will stress objectivity, it will remain true that just about everything we come to know will maintain some residue of feeling. Many people never develop a passion for mathematics or for music, for example, because that whole area of learning is subtly colored by the personality and attitudes of a teacher; whereas some of us have found just the opposite to be true: The passions of our lives are somehow derived from the enthusiasm and goodness of those who modeled an interest in math or music as a way of being happy and fulfilled. Thus our image of music or math includes some residue of the feelings we had when we first "fell in love" with the discipline.

The Function of Fantasy

Because imagery is deeper than logic or words, it allows interactions among its contents that are fluid and fertile, chaotic and creative. We know these interactions as the common phenomena of daydreams and musings and fantasies. States of fantasy make up a big part of each person's life. Psychologist Eric Klinger believes that a person's daydreams and fantasies contribute powerfully to the "inner flavor of a human personality"; in addition, they help to shape the structures of what a person considers meaningful, worthwhile and interesting.[6] The images that appear in fantasies include feelings, desires and hopes as well as the representations of objects. The purpose of fantasy is to help us maintain a sense of the "self." For each of us, our idea of "self" is made up of a number of "subselves." We identify in different regions of life with different models whom we admire and whose characteristics we try to make our own. In our fantasies, we try out responses to the things we fear and the things we hope for, building up and sustaining our own complex of "self" and "subselves."[7] One's sense of individual specialness and one's feeling of having a continuous life history come from this work of fantasy.

Such fantasy and reverie also allow us to deal with anger and the anticipation of pain. With children, these fantasies spill over into play. Jean Piaget notes that emotional conflicts reappear in symbolic play as a child recreates with dolls or toys a turbulent scene at the dinner table some hours before.[8] We can see how the imagination serves as a survival technique. The functioning of the imagination helps to maintain an inner equilibrium, balancing the impact of the physical world with the feeling-filled response of the world of imagination.

There are two additional functions of fantasy: Fantasy creates an ecology of purpose and it opens the scope for creativity. The themes of the imagination provide a basic sense of direction for the whole conscious life of the person. "The movement of images in awareness, particularly through repeated fantasy sequences, can inject a directionality into conceptual thinking. This directionality will eventually influence both the individual's self-integration and the construction of an objective world view."[9] Additionally, the processes of creativity depend fundamentally upon the fluid interplay of images at work in reverie and fantasy.

In summary, then, the world of images arises out of the need to maintain contact with moments of life that are important, beginning with the moment of birth. When life forces us to move beyond infantile dependencies and to give ourselves to other and new moments of reality, our images conserve both traces of our experience and a memory of the emotional tone of our history with these persons and objects. Imagination exists in order to maintain an equilibrium between inner conscious abilities and the outside environment. This balancing allows us to survive as a self (with our own self-understanding and expectations of ourselves) and to tune our desires into the available reality of our environment. In this way we can approach objectivity in sharing a world with others.

One of the most important purposes of imagination is its affirmation of the uniqueness of the individual. This sense of uniqueness derives from the links of origin, belonging and love that are among the most powerful elements in the repertory of mental images.[10] We are unique because we are loved, and we coexist in a world shared with those who give us this gift of love.

The realm of imagination is reality in hiding. All that we know, we know in deeper, richer, hidden ways beneath the threshold of language and words. One of the surprising dimensions of contemporary culture is its pragmatic attempts to influence attitudes and behavior not only by logical arguments and words, but also by direct raids upon the subsurface of our knowing. The so-called "subliminal" communication of the visual arts and music aims at breaking and entering the realm of imagination without first knocking at the door of rational discussion.

Culture, Community and Church

How does the culture of the family, the community and the church shape the imaginative world of the child? So far we have seen that imagination is the ground of knowing: It is the repository of objects, feelings and desires that have made us into the special beings that we are. It is also the magnetic field against which feelings for the good and evil of reality are measured and savored. Imagination has this power because, like the tide in an ocean of desire, it is capable of moving our dreams and our hopes toward peaceful communion with God, known as the ultimate harbor of love and safety.

Nothing is so difficult to grasp in the realm of imagination as the idea of God. In theology, we speak of God as our origin and our destiny: where we came from and where we hope to rest. In psychoanalytic terms, however, there is no difference for the infant between "mother" and "God." For the infant, mother is infinite abundance, perfect love, simple goodness. Even after this child discovers that mother is other than self and that mother can be negligent enough not to respond immediately upon request, "destiny" is still conceived of as hope for reunion with mother—fusion with primordial abundance. All through life, even when as growing "theologians" we incorporate more and more of the biblical, cultural and religious data of our communities, we must deal with the original agenda—the nostalgic dream of surrender to the first symbol of God who was mother. If we have reason to react negatively to what was predominantly inadequate parenting, we will somehow have to deal with that subliminal ache not only in our feelings about God, but also in our ideas and theology.

Quite significantly, then, the agenda for religious imagination comes from two sources: from biology and from revelation. It comes first from biology, because each of us must learn, step by step, how to make our way courageously through the journey that leads from dependency to generativity. We are born dependent; we grow into generative beings. All along the way we are challenged to rethink our self-understanding and to let go of patterns of behavior that we have gradually outgrown. Because we are sure only about the past we have known, we tend to be regressive in our search for security. At the same time, we are impatient for stimulation and eager for new experience. In this (psychoanalytic) frame of reference, the transcendent is always in the past. The overwhelming feeling of abundance that comes from mother as the source of our original comfort, as the only source of cosmic unity that we have ever experienced, is never matched in power or intensity.

On the other hand, the agenda for religious imagination that comes from revelation is radically different. It is oriented toward the future. God invites us to become new beings. The imagery of promise, of love and of fulfillment given in the scriptures intersects with the experiences rooted in our history and coded in our own imagination. The efficacy of God's proclamation somehow rides upon the readiness of our symbolic life to interpret as good news the proclamation of the divine promises.[11]

Paul Philibert

Symbolic Landscaping

How do we influence the functions of imagination through symbols? The image of "landscaping" can prove helpful. Just as the environment in which we live is designed and intended to give us a feeling of beauty and pleasure in our surroundings, so also is our psychic environment shaped by symbols. In our yards and gardens, we plant shade trees, flowering bushes, and beds of ornamental plants; a house or apartment is not complete until we adapt it to our wishes and make it our "home." Sometimes our landscaping means making do with something already there, like a large oak, an immense boulder, a structural support. Then we design around the available and the inescapable. All the same, by landscaping, we accept and integrate such elements into an overall plan which is our plan.

In our psychic life, the meanings of ordinary conversations and habitual actions are related to and interact with the "deep structure" of our imagination. This field of imagination is the yard or garden where our symbols flourish. Some of these have an archaic quality, leading us back to fundamental relations and stories that come from the earliest interactions with our parents. Other images play an important role because they parallel these archaic materials. As noted above, there is a constant interplay between the world of words and the subliminal world of imagination. The landscaping of that terrain of images is obviously of enormous significance, for it influences our readiness to understand the world of God and religion as well as the feelings that we invest in that world when it is shared with us.

Some of our most enduring symbols are formed in the earliest years of life. "The most obvious fact about the human infant," says John Macmurray, "is [its] total helplessness. It has no power of locomotion, nor even of coordinated movement."[12] But this radical unadaptedness for a life of isolation is in fact an adaptedness to dependency upon an adult human being. The human infant "is made to be cared for . . . born into a love relationship which is inherently personal."[13] The infant's contentment is closely associated with the physical presence of the mother and her physical contact. "It seems impossible to account for [this] except as an expression of satisfaction in the relation itself." This is a need which is not simply biological, but personal. "And it is astonishing at what an early age a baby cries not because of any physiological distress, but because [it] has noticed that [it] is alone, and is upset by [its] mother's absence."[14]

As we pay attention to these facts, it becomes clear that the relationship between mother and infant cannot be expressed exclusively in biological terms. Since the infant simply cannot live an isolated existence, the infant lives "a common life as one term in a personal relationship. Only in the process of development does [it] learn to achieve a relative independence, and that only by appropriating the techniques of a rational social tradition."[15]

A great deal depends upon how we interpret the meaning of this period of primordial life. Strong currents in our society would say that the infant at this point is prehuman. The worst aspect of various arguments in the abortion debate is the inclination to dehumanize the unborn child; it is often referred to as "fetal tissue." If, along those lines, we were to dismiss the significance of the infant's connection with its mother as merely the negative dynamic of its prerational incapacity, we would lose touch with a significant clue about our humanity. For, even though the human infant can live only through other people and in relation to them, it is fully a person. As Macmurray states, "[Its] rationality is already present, though only germinally, in the fact that [it] lives and can only live by communication. [Its] essential natural endowment is the impulse to communicate with another human being."[16]

When we accept the essential humanness of the infant, we recognize that our status as persons is not based upon individual rationality or even upon our exploits as rational beings, but is rather based upon our relatedness to others in radical interdependence. "[W]e are persons not by individual right, but in virtue of our relation to one another. . . . The unit of the personal is not the 'I', but the 'You and I.'"[17]

The Symbolic Agenda

Clearly the mother exercises a powerful symbolic force in the imagination of the child. She is the infant's security. The child's nutrition and physical well-being are totally dependent upon the mother as the giver of security and the protector of life. But the mother also is the infant's object of devotion. John

Gleason has spelled out the dynamics of this sacred relation between mother and infant as follows:

> When the baby gets hungry, it cries. Mother-god is all powerful (omnipotent) in the sense that she has it easily within her grasp to provide nourishment. . . . Through the preponderance of pleasurable or discomfiting experiences of Mother-god's uses of power, the child is learning a feeling-level lesson: Mother-god uses her power to make me feel happy, or Mother-god uses her power to make me feel angry, uncomfortable, and unhappy.[18]

While Gleason's suggestion is graphic, it must be stressed that we are talking about the structure of feelings that are coded into the realm of imagination, not about phrases the child says to itself. Yet, even though the child has not yet learned speech and clear reasoning, these feelings are registered as enduring products of its relation to mother as a symbol of the sacred.

Dr. Rene Spitz has observed that around three months of age, the infant learns to respond to the presence of a human face with a smile. The child will smile even at a drawn design of a face. So strong is this movement toward an interpersonal reaction that Spitz calls this mirroring of the human smile the primary organizer of the personality.[19] James Loder comments that this interpersonal exchange of smiles is a primal symbol of wholeness. He says, "I suggest that what is established in the original face-to-face interaction is the child's sense of personhood and a universal prototype of the Divine Presence. . . . (Here) the child seeks a cosmic-ordering, self-confirming impact from the presence of a loving other."[20]

In view of this analysis, these infantile experiences, along with their symbolic impact on the remainder of life, are not regressive; that is, they do not hold the infant back from development into an independent person. As we examine the descriptions of this phenomenon, we note the dynamics of what must be called "infantile contemplation." Neither for the infant nor for the mother is the interrelation or the interpersonal exchange a moment of panic or anxiety. It is one of the purest examples of total human trust and of emotional and personal self-giving. It is not only a symbolic paradigm, but also a moral and religious paradigm for the universal, human experience of transcendent fulfillment.

It would be useful to visit some of the other primary relations in the infant's life: the roles of the father, siblings, grandparents and the extended family are of great importance in supporting the child and extending its sense of connectedness to a larger world. Excellent research has been done by Antoine Vergote and Alvaro Tamayo on the influence of parents on children's representations of God. These authors conclude that the mother, as the first object of attachment, "remains the figure that primarily represents unconditional and confident love." The father thus makes a contribution that is absolutely necessary, because "the absence of law and authority generates a feeling of fundamental insecurity. . . . A father who makes no demands is experienced as a father who does not care for what the child will become."[21]

Stories and Revelation

But children do not live by emotions alone. They live by stories as well. Their natural curiosity impels them to enter the narrative world of their parents and their communities. They learn our stories and rework the meaning of their lives by fitting themselves inside the descriptions of the world that are given to them.

Observing parents in the process of teaching their infants to talk can be the source of important insights. The first efforts at speech are directed toward names that bind the child in relation to its parents and its family. Language functions as a system of belonging. Christian families introduce quite early the names of God and of Jesus and the stories of creation and redemption. This occurs naturally enough when there are older children in the family who already participate in family prayer and parish worship. The small child is eager to be included in the activities of the older members of the family, and as it grows in language skills its sharing of ritual language and gestures achieves just that.

Through teaching and churchgoing, children come to belong to the story of Jesus. Prayers in the family circle, the creche at Christmas, and the celebration of Christian holidays extend the structure of Christian meaning into the whole of their lives.

There is a charming passage in Sigrid Undset's novel, *Kristin Lavransdatter* (set in medieval Norway), in which the small Kristin is traveling with her father from her isolated farm to the big city of Hamar. In this incident, Kristin is left in the care of a kindly monk as her father goes off to visit with the bishop. Brother Edvin takes her into the church to admire the beautiful works of art that are being built there:

> But now Brother Edvin must go to the church, he said, and Kristin should go with him. . . . They were still building at this church as well, so that here, too, there stood a tall scaffolding in the cross where nave and transepts met. . . . First he climbed up a ladder and laid some boards straight up there, and then he came down again and helped the child up with him.
>
> Upon the greystone wall above her Kristin saw wondrous fluttering flecks of light; red as blood and yellow as beer, blue and brown and green. She would have turned to look behind her, but the monk whispered, "Turn not about." But when they stood together high upon the planking, he turned her gently round, and Kristin saw a sight so fair she almost lost her breath.
>
> Right over against her on the nave's south wall stood a picture, and it shone as if it were made of naught but gleaming precious stones. The many-hued flecks of light upon the wall came from rays which stood out from that picture; she herself and the monk stood in the midst of the glory. . . .
>
> 'Twas like standing far off and looking into the heavenly kingdom. Behind a network of black streaks, she made out little by little the Lord Christ Himself in the most precious of red robes, the Virgin Mary in raiment blue as heaven, holy men and maidens in shining yellow and green and violet array. . . .
>
> "Stand here," [Brother Edvin] whispered, "and [it will] shine right upon you from Christ's own robe."[22]

This enchanting scene was a moment of awakening for Kristin. In order for her to be deeply touched by the bath of bloody color coming from the robe of Christ, she had to bring the story of Jesus from her imagination to the figure of the Christ in the window. Then the visual splendor of the stained glass transfigured her inner feelings of faith. The sparkling color of this Christ figure in the church window became part of her frame of reference for the glory and the goodness of God. Her childhood trip to Hamar remained a life-giving memory for her for the rest of her days. Such religious experiences become marker events that can be pointed to as moments when "God came unmistakably close."

All children have such moments—or ought to have. To translate creeds and liturgical texts into convincing reality takes time and patient love.

Father Joseph Gallagher shows us another side of raising young people in Catholic faith in these passages from his autobiography:

> When a youngster was once told to say two Our Fathers for his penance, he pleaded, "But I only know one." Youngsters have long been the best brighteners of confessional darkness, especially with their well-intentioned variations on traditional formulas for confessing and making the Act of Contrition. A composite of such variations might go like this:
>
> Penitent: "Blast me, Father, for I have sins. This is my last confession . . . since a month ago. I said 'Damn it' four times — three times before, and once just now. I ate meat on Friday."
>
> Priest: "Anything else?"
>
> Penitent: "Oh yes: potatoes and gravy and corn. I am sorry for these and all the sins of my fast life."
>
> Priest: "All right. Now make a good act of contrition."
>
> Penitent: "A Good Act of Contrition — O my God I am hardly sorry for having defended Thee . . . and I test all my sins because I dread the laws of heaven. . . . I firmly dissolve to help Thy grace to do the penance and to end my life. Amen."[23]

Illuminating Moments

Living between the cosmic yearning of the imagination and the confusing requirements of a demanding world is stressful much of the time. It is not surprising that many people have experiences of breakthrough that allow them to sense the reality of life and the awesomeness of their own reality. An elderly English gentleman, reflecting on his youth, tells this story:

> During the year when I was eight another important event happened to me. As I stood dressed to go out [on a walk], I was actually thinking and considering my position, something like this — 'Here I am, a little boy of seven; I wonder where I was eight years ago.' At that tremendous thought I stood rooted to the carpet . . . with a wave of tremendous feeling sweeping over me. I suddenly felt old and aware of being somebody very ancient, weighed by Time, of almost unbeginning individuality. Eight years ago, I thought: why not eighty or eight hundred? I felt ancient and old and full of Time. Nowadays, of course, I cannot find the wording to state clearly what I mean. I remember it quite exactly, nevertheless.[24]

P a u l   P h i l i b e r t

The Church's Ritual Wisdom

The marvel of our Christian liturgy, of course, is that it binds up our inner needs with the symbols of God's presence and love. If our deepest inner need is a voracious hunger for affirmation and meaning, this is met in countless ways in the material, verbal, musical and ritual signs that have erupted within the church as a community of faith through the centuries.

The child's nostalgia for being lovingly touched by the cosmic mother lives on in us. The church meets that nostalgia with washing, anointing, embracing, laying on hands, and gestures of reverence like prostrations. These gestures have a symbolic resonance that can touch the depths of our yearning.

The young person's hope to be included, to be loved as precious in the competitive, emotional environment of the family or the schoolroom lives on, too. The church meets that hope by choosing and calling, commissioning for service, including in corporate action, and signing with the sign of the cross.

The youth's desire to be recognized as unique, to be known as that never-before-appearing presence that is the emerging self, lives on as well. The church meets that desire by setting one apart for leadership, cherishing one's gifts, and opening space for new expressions of life.

The church has these treasures. That's true. The awkward fact, however, is that not all ministers and not all faithful people know about this. Vulnerable ourselves to the impact of the popular culture, we ministers often celebrate our Christian rites with efficient detachment. Louis Weil calls this the "victory of verbalism" that has led some priests to become fixated upon rigid performance of a text, without consideration for affective and intuitive reading of the pastoral situation.[25] Couple this with the competition of the mass media for the minds and hearts of ourselves and our children and it is not so surprising to find so few young people in our churches.

The Struggle for Control over the Imagination

Once again I return to the overwhelming influence of the media on our popular culture. In trying to understand how we got to where we are, it may help to see the media culture as a monstrous caricature of the principles of the American revolution. If the eighteenth century and the Victorian era were straightlaced and repressive, the media culture is permissive—to the point of seeming a pep rally for impulsive release. One can watch MTV as a clearing-house of popular images, to see what is the latest assault upon taste and impulsive constraints. This is supposedly liberating us from the servitude of tradition.

If the European monarchies were elitist, then the popular culture must exalt the voice of the unsophisticated. Archie Bunker was one thing (we could all see ourselves in Archie Bunker). But public television apart, one would guess that many American television personalities learned their manners at a Kentucky stud farm. If religious leaders were Puritanical or Jansenistic, then the popular culture sees its role as to unmask their hypocrisy—to eradicate their influence.

It is clear, however, that the real motive for the media is not fairness but money, not philosophy but power, not equality but profit. Social psychology has known for three decades about the role of violence and sexual passion in engaging the imagination of the masses. Automobiles repeatedly advertise their machines with sexual innuendo not because the seat of a car is the most comfortable place to have sex, but because lust has become the common coin of the realm of social manipulation.

I suspect that few serious citizens would disagree that these aspects of the popular culture have polluted our symbolic ecology. Repetition is the key to internalization. The church used to have such ritual moments as the Angelus three times a day to reinforce the understanding of the mystery that our world is permeated by grace. Television uses advertising every ten minutes to reinforce the public's responsiveness to sponsors' greed.

As Michael Medved observes:

> You might think that you can say to yourself, "I'll just tune out the messages of the media," but it's not possible today. In the past, if you talked about popular culture, you meant going to a movie theatre perhaps once a week and paying your money to see a single show. But modern technological advances have brought us boom boxes and walkmans and VCRs, television and MTV. The messages, the images, are everywhere around us and seep into every corner of our lives.[26]

Paul Philibert

Responding from the Heart of the Church

In my treatment of the symbols above, I stressed the themes of security and the sacred. But there is another powerful symbolic theme that cannot be overlooked—sublimation. In the view of psychiatry, the rechanneling of vital energy away from forbidden areas and into approved areas of activity is an essential mechanism of cultural growth. Gross attachments to the objects of the libido—for example, the growing child clutching mother's skirts or the adolescent's self-indulgent autoeroticism—need to be redirected. In a similar way, countless spontaneous impulses become the terrain for sublimation. Sublimation as a theme, then, touches upon the symbols of those things that are worthy of investing in as adequate goals for living.

The church retells day by day the story of Jesus and its ramifications for his disciples and for the early Christian community as a way of holding up symbols for sublimation:

> Blessed are the poor.
> Blessed are the merciful.
> Blessed are those who hunger and thirst for justice.
> Love your neighbor as yourself.
> Come, follow me.

These and other sayings of Jesus become images for us of the real meaning of our human existence. We not only read these texts; we embody them in mutual interaction and celebrate that in our agape—a feast of joy and transformation.

It is clear that the church is locked into powerful competition with the popular culture for power over our imaginations. The scope of the popular culture is overwhelming and its means intrusive, particularly into the imaginative life of our children. Yet the means of the church are not negligible. It is, however, important for us to recognize how to invest them with the full vitality of which they are capable. It is a tragedy when a Catholic family returns from Sunday church-going with the feeling that they have just indulged in a meaningless exercise in placating a guilty conscience. Sunday celebration rests on a firm theological base: We belong to God. Making ordinary persons in ordinary families into God's community—the People of God—was God's idea. God is impatient for us to notice how overwhelmingly present is divine life in our midst. Pope John Paul II has written:

> The lay faithful are called to restore to creation all its original value. In ordering creation to the authentic well-being of humanity in an activity governed by the life of grace, they share in the exercise of the power with which the Risen Christ draws all things to himself.[27]

In the renewal of these last 30 years, the church has revived the faithful's appreciation of their destiny through the building of base communities in which it has become possible to liberate the power of faith and grace in their daily lives. The Rite of Christian Initiation of Adults has revitalized many parishes by expanding the understanding of "conversion" as the basic category of Christian experience, expanding it to become a dynamic that transforms everyone in the parish and the corporate climate of the parish itself.

The liturgical renewal of these decades has done much to improve the celebration of the rites. Through the improvement of texts, gestures and music, many assemblies now appear to be joyful rather than imprisoned. Even more, the liturgical renewal has stressed the revolving door between worship and work. We bring in the door "the joy and hope, the grief and anguish" of our ordinary world, to be offered and transformed in sacramental work at the table of the Lord; we take out the door the faith and spirit of the assembly to encounter once again our earthly dwelling place. The fruit of this awakening is an acceptance of a life of *diakonia*—a serving presence in and with the world in its painful crisis of change and transformation.

Instead of ending with a heavy heart, I propose that we see the encouraging possibilities that still exist. Our own celebrations are vehicles of grace. We believe that God has not given up in the struggle to manifest and incarnate: to let us see the divine and make us reveal the holy.

Our children are the key. They belong to the future. We, as their parents and teachers, have an awesome role in landscaping their religious imaginations. We don't need to do anything heroic to accomplish this (unless you feel that sustaining the demands of the ordinary in these times is heroic). But we do need to live the mystery of Christ and invite them to live it with us with as much fullness and joy as we can learn to celebrate.

Children demonstrate certain qualities of faith that are so essential to our Christian integrity that Jesus exaggerated the point:

Truly I tell you, unless you change and become like children, you will never
enter the kingdom of heaven. Whoever becomes humble like this child is the
greatest in the kingdom of heaven. Whoever welcomes one such child in my
name welcomes me. (Matthew 18:3–5)

We have seen some ways in which this saying of Jesus reverberates
through our explanation of the life of the imagination. Each infant's trust of
its mother is the foundational structure upon which a world of hope is
built.[28] The loving interrelation of infant and mother that I called infantile
contemplation is the point of departure for a history of transcendence.
Unless we value trust and contemplation as children do, there is no kingdom
of heaven for us.

The child's impulsive eagerness to share in life, to be part of the party,
has the capacity to regenerate our own dullness. When children's eyes
become large as saucers while listening to the old stories, they reveal for us
the power of story and rite to transform hearts.

Children also have an ability—at times—to linger, to rest in their
places of security: Grandma's house, Uncle Charley's den, special places—
especially someone's lap. Children thus become a symbol of communication through wholeness, a reminder of the reality of communication
through affectivity that is the knowledge of love.

Again, children have a pragmatic sense about events. "Show me; let me
do it!" they say, often enough. They find it unreasonable to be held captive
for an hour or more in a dimly lighted, closed room unless there is a story
to live, a meal to share, a work to be done. They can help us revivify
our mortally domesticated worship if we are brave enough to admit them as
full participants.

Louis Weil, again, summarizes the point:

The authentic inclusion of children in the normative models of parish liturgy
may work for the salvation of the adults—and certainly for their wholeness as
worshipers. For centuries a false liturgical mentality has tried to let us forget
that we have bodies, that we are physical persons, and that our worship
involves us with each other. . . . Children bring a naturalness to the liturgy
which stands as a judgment upon our overformalized routines. Until they are
pressed into behavioral molds, they bring a wonderful openness to the
experience of word and gesture, touch and movement—to the whole array of
elements which lie at the heart of the liturgical act.[29]

So maybe we can save our experience of church and survive. But as soon as I say that, I recognize that this is not God's way of talking. Remember Isaiah's experience of God speaking to him in his exile:

> It is not enough for you to be my servant, to restore the tribes of Jacob and bring back the survivors of Israel. I shall make you a light to the nations so that my salvation may reach to the remotest parts of the earth. (Isaiah 49:6)

God has made us chosen people, a sacramental people who say and do what God says and does in this world. Even in adversity, God goes on promising:

> Kings will stand up when they see,
> princes will see and bow low,
> because of Yahweh who is faithful,
> the Holy One of Israel who has chosen you. (Isaiah 49:7)

We are the parents and teachers and prophets of the children of promise. Let us believe in them. Let us rejoice in their promise.

Notes

[1] Michael Medved, "Popular Culture and the War Against Standards," *Journal of the American Family Association* (April 1991): 15.

[2] Ibid., 13.

[3] Mardi Horowitz, *Image Formation and Cognition* (New York: Appleton Century Crofts, 1970), 4–28.

[4] Matthias Neumann, OSB, "Toward an Integrated Theory of Imagination," *International Philosophical Quarterly* XVIII (1978): 258.

[5] Jean Piaget and Barbel Inhelder, *The Psychology of the Child* (New York: Basic Books, 1969), 28ff.

[6] Eric Klinger, *Structures and Functions of Fantasy* (New York: Wiley, 1971), 9–10. See Neumann, 264–5.

[7] Klinger, 352–6.

[8] Piaget and Inhelder, 60, note 4.

[9] Neumann, 267.

[10] Ibid., 274.

[11] Editor's note: The author explains this further in "Readiness for Ritual," in Regis A. Duffy, OFM, ed., *Alternative Futures for Worship*, vol. 1. (Collegeville: Liturgical Press, 1987), 63–121.

[12] John Macmurray, *Persons in Relation* (London: Faber and Faber, 1961), 47.

[13] Ibid., 48.

[14] Ibid., 49.

[15] Ibid., 50.

[16] Ibid., 51.

[17] Ibid., 61.

[18] John J. Gleason, Jr., *Growing Up to God* (Nashville: Abingdon, 1975), 26–27.

[19] Rene Spitz, *The First Year of Life* cited in James Loder, *The Transforming Moment* (San Francisco: Harper Row, 1981), 166.

[20] Ibid., 166–7.

[21] Antoine Vergote, "The Dynamics of the Family and Its Significance for Moral and Religious Development" in *Towards Moral and Religious Maturity* (Morristown NJ: Silver Burdett, 1980), 100–101. Cf. Antoine Vergote and Alvaro Tamayo, *The Parental Figures and the Representation of God* (The Hague: Mouton, 1981). Also, Anna-Maria Rizzuto, *The Birth of the Living God: A Psychoanalytical Study* (Chicago: University of Chicago Press, 1979).

[22] Sigrid Undset, *Kristin Lavransdatter* Vol. I: *The Bridal Wreath* (New York: Knopf, 1923; reprinted by Vintage Books, 1987), 29.

[23] Joseph Gallagher, *The Pain and the Privilege: The Diary of a City Priest* (Garden City NY: Image Books, 1983), 156.

[24] Edward Robinson, *The Original Vision: A Study of the Religious Experience of Childhood* (Oxford: Religious Experience Research Unit, 1977), 115. Cf. Andrew Greeley, *The Religious Imagination* (Los Angeles: Sadlier, 1981), 17: "Religion becomes a communal event when a person is able to link his own grace experience with the overarching experience of his religious tradition . . ., that is to say, when he perceives a link between his experience of grace and the tradition's experience of grace, when he becomes aware that there is a correspondence or a correlation between the resonating picture or story in his imagination and the story passed on by his religious heritage."

[25] Weil, 56–57.

[26] Medved, 15.

[27] John Paul II, *Christifideles Laici: Post-Synodal Apostolic Exhortation* (Boston: Daughters of St. Paul, 1989), no. 14.

[28] The theme of trust and hope as rooted in maternal security is also one of the building blocks of the Life-Cycle Theory of Erik Erikson. See, for example, his *Insight and Responsibility* (New York; Norton, 1964), chapter IV.

[29] Weil, 57.

Children in the Assembly of the Church

To think about children in the church is to think about the march of generations. After all, we who worry about our children were once children ourselves, and the parents who kept us in line were themselves once children in church, and so on back through the centuries. And one day, the children over whom we fuss and fret will be parents fussing and fretting about the lives, religious and otherwise, of their own children. When we think about children, therefore, we think about tradition: not as the dead hand of custom, but as the living, life-giving thread entrusted to us by those who have gone before us to pass on to those who come after us.

It is right that we should be concerned about the problems of passing this tradition on to our children, but we should probably expect less of ourselves and more of the Spirit of God, even in the matter of liturgical participation. A case in point:

My earliest memory of attending Mass derives from a time when I must have been about four or five. I was standing on the sponge-rubber kneeler, with my elbows resting on the top of the pew. People were packed in like sardines, or so it seemed. At our church in those days, a gong instead of a bell was struck to mark the solemn moments of the Mass. Sometimes

I could see the priest, and for a long time I thought there must be a button on the floor because the gong sounded at the exact moment his knee hit the floor. But what I remember best about the Mass in my earliest years in the pews (for I started serving Mass at five or six years of age, when Sister Scholastica had somehow taught a group of us to say *"Ad deum qui laetificat iuventutem meam"*) was the solemn silence of the consecration. Once the gong sounded for the *Hanc igitur,* the constant background noise of shuffles, sniffles, coughs, page-turnings, nose-blowings and so on came to an immediate stop. In a church of probably 400 people, you could have heard a pin drop. What you heard instead were the six strikes of the gong: three for the consecration of the bread, three more for the consecration of the cup, and the "silent" sound of 400 heads stretching up for a glimpse of the sacred species. And hardly had the last gong sounded when the dam was burst and a flood of coughing, sniffling, shuffling and nose-blowing rolled over the kneeling congregation. I have to confess that my first memory of playing an active and conscious role in the liturgy was that of trying to be the first to cough, and thus the first to break the silence, as the priest rose from his genuflection and turned the page to the *Unde et memores.*

Still, it is not my intention to approach this topic from the nose-over-the-pew perspective of the child. Instead, I make bold to ask, "What does the presence of children at the liturgy do for the church?" Not "Should we have liturgies for children, or liturgies of the word for children?" nor "What can we do for children at liturgy?" Elsewhere in this volume Paul Philibert writes of the church in the imaginative landscape of the child. I will reflect on the child in the imaginative landscape of the church. How do we see them there, and what do they mean to us?

One caveat. I have just been referring to children at Mass, but the title of this chapter is "Children in the Assembly of the Church." There is a difference. Most parishes have Masses; few really have an assembly of the local church. Masses are multiplied to meet the demands of numbers or merely for convenience, but the ideal liturgical assembly is a gathering of all God's people in a given place: men, women, children, the elderly, the sick, representatives of every social group and social stratum. This is the church most visible as what she is: the work of Christ, gathering the scattered children of God into one. For most of its history the church resisted the multiplication of Masses. Even as late as the nineteenth century, it would have been thought very odd, on the whole, for most parishes to have more than one Mass, since the Mass by definition had always been understood as primarily the worship offered by the entire people. There is a whole biblical theology behind the concept of the assembly, a theology that would have enormous practical implications if it were ever again taken seriously, but that is the subject for another paper.[1] Suffice it to say that the typical congregation at Mass is not usually an assembly in the full sense of the term; nevertheless, my focus will be on the ideal of the assembly and children's place within it.

After a look at the tradition and the role children played in our liturgy in the past, this paper will examine the presence of children at liturgy today, especially from the perspective of their symbolic value. In conclusion, I will offer some personal reflections, not all derived directly from the preceding, on practical matters of children at liturgy.

The Tradition

Children in the Liturgy

The matter is not often discussed in general treatments of the history of the liturgy,[2] or even in studies of the history of the Christian initiation of children, but the fact is that children played a significant, indeed often prominent role in the church's liturgy from late antiquity until modern times. To qualify that, it is more accurate to speak of young boys playing such roles, though in monasteries of religious women, young girls also exercised liturgical functions, at least in the choir.[3]

The modern altar server and the rare phenomenon of the boys choir—though the latter still flourishes in the famous choir schools of England—are merely lingering vestiges of a long-established tradition that accorded liturgical roles to young boys. The practice dates from at least the fourth century, when boys were not only entrusted with the ministries of singing and reading in the liturgical assembly, but, were actually ordained for such tasks. Perhaps as early as the fifth century the need to train these children for their liturgical roles, as well as to ensure their general education, led to the establishment in Rome of various choir schools attached to Roman basilicas.[4]

In the early centuries, of course, the liturgical chants were little more than cantillations, thus not very different from the tones used for the proclamation of the readings. Indeed, what we call the "responsorial psalm" was often counted as a reading. In any case, the liturgical function of public reading and singing seems to have been in place by the fifth century, when various choir schools, attached to the city's basilicas, were established at Rome.[5] The practice spread, and in Gaul these children were accommodated as members of the bishop's household and given the tonsure at the age of seven, making them junior members of the clergy. Once they could read, they could be ordained as lectors.[6] Later they might be ordained as psalmists to sing the responsorial psalm, or as acolytes for the service of the altar. Though generally the children were seven or older, there are some instances of children as young as four or five serving in such roles. Once they reached adolescence they might return to the world or pursue their ecclesiastical studies, taking over new responsibilities in the life of the local church.

In medieval Europe this practice continued to flourish, with children being given to the church by their parents to be schooled in the arts and to serve God in the liturgy. The main centers for this were the cathedrals and great abbeys,[7] where as few as five or six boys or as many as twenty were housed and trained to sustain the daily round of prayer. Besides serving as choristers and readers, they also assumed responsibilities as cross-bearers and thurifers (if they were in acolyte's orders) or as candle-bearers and water-bearers. They would also hold the book for the priest presiding at the office.

These offices could take up most of the day, especially when additional offices of the dead or of the Blessed Virgin were added, and systems of rotation were introduced to allow boys to keep up with their school work, while the youngest boys were generally excused from the night offices.

The numbers of children living this sort of life were never very large. One estimate suggests there may have been 1,500 boys being maintained by cathedrals, abbeys, collegiate churches and the larger parish churches for the sake of the divine liturgy.[8] Nonetheless, it is important to stand back from this phenomenon and ask its significance. Some may argue that it is simply an historical curiosity of no great importance. Or one could see it perhaps as an early form of the seminary system, for it is certainly true that being accepted as a boy chorister was for many the first step on a long ladder of ecclesiastical promotion;[9] a few early medieval popes began their careers in the schola cantorum of the Lateran.[10] Or one could look at the matter in purely pragmatic terms. It has been suggested, for example, that the reason children were chosen as readers and chanters was that their clear, high voices carried well in basilicas and churches.[11] I suspect this doesn't fully explain the practice, which is related to the way children were viewed in the ancient and medieval worlds.

The Place of Children in Society

Our ancestors probably felt a certain amount of ambivalence about children: They loved them, but dared not invest too much in them because they frequently died young. They often treated them like pets, with a mixture of affection, cruelty and sheer neglect. What makes our distant ancestors very different from us in this respect is that they spent far less time studying children and thinking about children and providing for children than we do. Nonetheless, their children did have a place in public worship.

Well before Christian liturgy developed, there were cultic traditions in the ancient world which offered extensive possibilities for the participation of young children. In the city-states of ancient Greece, schools had long been established to train the children of noble families to sing the ritual chants at state festivals. At Rome, where the oldest religious cults were those of the family, the younger children of the household had indispensable roles in the offering of sacrifice.[12] These domestic rites may well have provided models for the development of civic rites and public sacrifices, for here, too, boys were required—"boys of free birth whose fathers and mothers were still alive"—to exercise certain ritual functions, assisting the high priest. Among the specific roles attributed to them were carrying and holding vessels of food and water. Following the Greek example, young boys and girls also came to sing in the chorus at Roman state religious functions, and did so well into the Christian era.[13]

Thus the historical tradition of choristers and altar boys has its roots deep in pre-Christian antiquity. While no direct connection can be established between Christian and pre-Christian practice, it is only to be expected that, if Christians established choirs of children to sing at public worship, it was because they shared the same sort of cultural suppositions as their pre-Christian ancestors. Closer examination of this early mindset is enlightening.

I referred earlier to the ambivalence with which children seem to have been treated in the ancient world. They tended generally to be viewed as defective adults. The norm of what it was to be human was represented by the male of the species, especially by the successful public figure or the head of the household. All other persons in society were measured in terms of this standard. Thus slaves were not fully human because they did not possess the freedom of self-determination. Women were often regarded as coming close to the fulness of humanity, but their social and legal dependence on fathers and husbands kept them mostly in the second rank. Like women, slaves, the elderly and the handicapped, children were excluded from the political process and lacked social influence. In short, in relation to the norm, they were all marginal.

Infants represented an extreme case: Born without the gift of speech or reason or discernment, they were not regarded as really human at all. Not yet. It was the prerogative of the head of the family to decide whether to keep or abandon a newborn infant. If kept, it was not named for a week, for so many died in the first days of life. Once named, it was regarded somewhat as a handicapped person; the very word "infant" means one who cannot speak. With time, of course, that handicap would be overcome, and the infant would grow to be a child and then a youth. As a youth, he nevertheless was still defective, for he was not yet able to fight battles on behalf of the city, any more than the women and the elderly and the handicapped. He was not yet a man.

Thus, children were generally regarded as incomplete social beings, at best persons-in-progress. This very lack of humanity also meant that they were regarded as closer to the nonhuman world, the invisible world, the supernatural world. Not only were they recent arrivals from that other world, but their precarious hold on human life meant they were always liable to slip back there. Though born, they were not fully of this world and they only became fully of this world if they survived and grew and became powerful in the world. Thus one scholar has written:

> Classical society saw children as especially associated with the divine world because they were unimportant, not because they were the same as adults: the child may serve as an acolyte just because he is not an adult, he is not really there.[14]

Or again:

> Whatever the exact role of children in the various mystery cults, in general the presence of children at the pagan religious ceremonies of Roman families and of the Roman communities was not a sign of the equality of the child and the adult, but a sign that the child only marginally belonged to the human community. It was because the child "did not count," was in a sense "not there" as a citizen, that the child could be used to assist at ceremonies, and that the child's words could be taken as ominous, mediating between the divine world and the human.[15]

Children in Christian Society

In many respects the Jews, and then the Christians, took a strong, unyielding stand against the attitudes of the age, not least where newborns and the treatment of young children were concerned. Both Jews and Christians, for example, refused abortion and still more adamantly repudiated the common practice of simply abandoning unwanted children.[16] The child was treated as a human being.

The Christian community went still further, for infants could be baptized, confirmed and admitted to the eucharist, just like adults. In the communion of the baptized there was a radical unity and equality in which the normal social distinctions between male and female, Jew and Greek, slaves and free, even children and adults, simply failed to count. Unfortunately, as we know all too well, the radical new order ushered in by water and the Spirit was quickly compromised and within a generation or two socially accepted principles of hierarchical living penetrated the community of the baptized, too. But it would be several hundred years before infants were marginalized by the church and made second-rate Christians: baptized at birth, but not confirmed and admitted to eucharist until infancy and early childhood were over.

On the other hand, something of the otherworldliness of the child survived in Christian mentalities, too. Just as children's sayings were often taken as utterances of other-worldly wisdom in pagan Greece and Rome, so in Christianity.[17] It was a child at Milan who first shouted "Ambrose for Bishop!" The cry was taken as a sign from heaven by the crowd, who took up the chant and prevailed upon the clergy to elect the catechumen, Ambrose, then governor of the city, as its next bishop. In one of the most familiar scenes in Christian history, Augustine is walking in his garden, overcome with remorse for his past sins. To tell the story in his own words:

> And, lo, I heard from a nearby house, a voice like that of a boy or girl, I know not which, chanting and repeating over and over, "Take up and read. Take up and read." Instantly, with altered countenance, I began to think most intently whether children made use of any such chant in any kind of game, but I could not recall hearing it anywhere. I checked the flow of my tears and got up, for I interpreted this solely as a command given me by God to open the book and read the first chapter I should come upon.[18]

He seized the New Testament, opened it at Romans 13:13–14, and the rest, as they say, is history.

Examples of this kind can be multiplied: child oracles, child miracle workers, child martyrs—all the way back to the infancy of Jesus and the tragedy of the Holy Innocents. It is precisely the "otherness" of children that makes them special and enables them to serve as efficacious symbols of the links between this world and the world unseen. They represent the lowest rungs on the ladder of worldly success and achievement, so they are at the opposite end of the scale from the secure and the powerful. One expression of this symbolic opposition between child and adult is to be found in all those traditions that lasted through the middle ages, but which also survived in some places until modern times, namely the "rites of reversal" associated with the feast of St. Nicholas, or Holy Innocents' Day, where the boy choristers would elect one of their number to be bishop for a day. He in turn would choose from among his fellows those who were to be the chancellor and chaplains and so on. Not only did the boy bishop preside at the daily round of prayer for that day and preach a sermon to the people, but the senior clergy, reversing their roles, became the choristers, acolytes, book-bearers and water-bearers. In monasteries of religious women the same reversals were effected, with one of the young girls in the monastery school taking over as abbess.[19]

Most of these practices are now extinct, but they were once a lively part of our tradition, and reflected the place accorded to children in the collective Christian imagination. If they were assigned ministries in the liturgy it was less for practical than for symbolic reasons. It was because they were seen as standing closer to the veil that divides the visible from the invisible, the temporal order from the eternal. Compared to the high and the mighty, they represented the opposite end of the human spectrum in an assembly which, to be truly Catholic, should represent all degrees and conditions of humanity.

But there is something else to learn from this history, something about the liturgy itself. It was regarded as the public worship of God, to be offered day and night in the name of the whole people, in season and out of season, according to the rhythm of feasts, fasts, and festivals of the Christian year, and according to the round of public prayer that hallowed the succession of days and nights.

Obviously there is no going back to the middle ages and no sense in supposing Christians in any great numbers are going to start singing the liturgy of the hours appointed for the different phases of the day, but we do need to ask whether, in accommodating what is left of our liturgy to the convenience of a commuting public, we have not reversed the priorities of prayer. Choristers were needed because it was taken for granted that great churches would echo every day with the praises of God. Today we simply do not think in terms of the parish as having for its primary purpose the offering of continuous prayer and praise to God. We have tended to reverse the priorities: The choir is less for the glory of God than for the sake of the people; the adaptations made for the children are justified on grounds of their educational value, not because children have a right to praise and pray alongside us. If our ancestors turned cathedrals over to children, it was because they knew in some profound way that the real world is the opposite of the one we take for granted.

To summarize, then: Children have been significantly present in the liturgical assembly from earliest times and have always been entrusted with significant roles, whether it be that of the fourth-century lector, the twelfth-century chorister or the twentieth-century altar server. Yet the motivations for assigning these roles to children lay less in a desire to give the children something to do than in the recognition that, while children are part of the community of the baptized, they represent values other than those represented by adult members of the community. The adults were not there for the sake of the children nor the children for sake of the adults, but both were there to play their assigned roles in celebrating the God of all humanity. Thus, while children have played a long and significant role in the assembly of the church, the tradition shows them in a rather different light than do the practices of our own assemblies.

The Place of Children in the Assembly

In his book *Congregation: Stories and Structures,* James F. Hopewell writes about symbols of congregational identity, those elements that give each parish its special feel and special meanings. Each parish, he states, has its own feel, its own flavor, its own character. It is hard to put a finger on what sorts of things create such a sense of identity, but Hopewell suggests that some features of parish life and practice act as symbols, recognizable to the parishioners, but not to others. He points out that such symbols are deeply rooted in the collective psyche, but that there is no necessarily conscious, still less agreed, understanding of the meanings of such symbols because "Members are quick to champion, but slow to explain, the symbols of their identity."[20] How often have we heard: "We've always done it this way"? We are attached to arrangements and practices, but cannot say why.

In any case, many of these symbols are not specifically religious. They may have to do with traffic patterns, with how news is circulated, with how the pews are arranged or occupied, with what sorts of people get to do what sorts of jobs. Hopewell cites two particularly important examples of what he means by these identity-creating symbols: money and children.

Money is "frequently an emotion-laden metaphor that both expresses and provokes the identity of a specific congregation."[21] Hopewell points out that some parishes worry about money all the time; another parish will treat it as an unmentionable, rarely raising the topic and then with disdain; in another parish the taking up of the collection—and maybe a second and third collection—is a time-consuming public performance. His point is that money is never just about money: Money is a symbol around which many parochial images, meanings and values cluster to create the specific identity of a parish. Note that such a symbol, emotional and powerful as it may be, is only one of a cluster of such symbols, and that it can play quite different roles in different parishes and congregations.

> Another world symbol in congregational idiom is children, also an emotion-laden metaphor. Different churches treat their children in different symbolic ways. One secrets them in soundproof rooms and becomes uncomfortable if too many appear in the sanctuary.[22] A neighboring congregation, exposing its fecundity, arranges the public display of its children at worship. Another church nearby devises creative campaigns to attract more young people and families with children, while yet another acknowledges the absence of children as it grieves its own aging.[23]

Out of its own unique combination of such symbols, Hopewell argues, each congregation fashions its identity. I know of no formal research that has ever been done on this topic, but it is possible to draw upon one's own experience of different congregations.[24]

Children Not Welcome Here

There are congregations, for example, that are simply hostile to children. I rarely go to Saturday evening Mass, because it seems to me a rather esoteric idea that Sunday begins in our calendar, as the sabbath begins in the Jewish calendar, on the previous afternoon. Nonetheless, some domestic requirement made it necessary on one occasion, and I took my two-year old daughter with me. She was just learning to talk. She did not sleep through the liturgy, but neither did she create mayhem. Nonetheless, throughout the liturgy the elderly couple in front of me turned around repeatedly to give disapproving frowns at fairly regular intervals. This was aimed at me talking to Anna in a low whisper, pointing things out to her to help engage her with what was going on. In any case, things progressed and we reached the kiss of peace. I shook hands with the people to left and right and behind, but the couple in front adamantly refused to turn round for just this once. Feeling the alienation, I tapped the gentleman on the shoulder and said "Peace." "Go to hell," he said.

I have no doubt that the experience of children being unwelcome in certain parishes or at certain liturgies is very common. Cry rooms, for example, are highly ambivalent in this regard. Creating sound-proof cry rooms can be a genuine service to parents with restless children, but insisting that all young children be taken there simply says that children are unwelcome in the assembly of the faithful.

Children on Parade

At the other extreme there are those churches and those congregations that like to parade their children, and regularly celebrate child-centered liturgies. I emphasize once again that I am not referring to liturgies specifically for children, but about the Sunday assembly and the role of children in it. The question is whether children belong there and how.

There are liturgies, then, in which, one way or another, the focus is on the children. Children are not only heard, but seen: the children's choir, the child altar servers (boys and girls), child readers, child gift-bearers, even children ministering communion. There may be a children's sermon, perhaps with the children summoned out of the congregation to sit in the sanctuary and look coy. Such a focus on children can transpire in one or more of three ways:

a. There are liturgies in which the main focus is the children's sermon. This happens occasionally in Catholic churches, but in my limited experience it is the Presbyterians who have done most to make this a regular feature of Sunday worship. They will usually include a children's sermon as well as an adult sermon in the same service. What I have invariably noticed about such sermons, however, is that they are not so much addressed to the children, as addressed to the grown-ups through the children. Often, the preacher will ask questions or make remarks to the children while looking to get a reaction from the adult audience.

b. There are liturgies in which parents put their children on parade. One thinks of children making up the offertory procession, or children's choirs, or being chosen as May queen or her bridesmaids. First communions and confirmations also lend themselves to this sort of display, which seems not altogether unconnected with similar phenomena in the wider culture. If the President and Mrs. Clinton come to town, they will invariably be greeted by two exceedingly cute little girls who will present them with a bouquet. If they need a bouquet, why doesn't an adult present it? Or one may think of the practice of having small boys and girls dressed to the nines to throw flower petals at weddings. These examples are performances in which the ideas, the initiative, the procedure, the dress and the decorum are all imposed on the children by excited and anxious parents. It is not all that big a jump from having Suzie chosen as a bridesmaid to having Suzie entered in a baton-twirling contest or a junior Miss America beauty contest. Note that the children are again being manipulated by adults for the entertainment or ego-building of adults. They play a sort of vicarious role: Children are chosen for the part because if they succeed, that is marvelous and reflects glory on the parents; whereas if they make a mistake, well, they are only children. It is as if, through their children, adults pursue the glory of public roles, while minimizing the risks of losing face. Is that one of the possible reasons for parading children in the liturgy, too?

c. Third, there are the attempts to accommodate the liturgy to children, ranging from the selection of the children's eucharistic prayers or simplified readings and childish songs, to the outright transformation of the liturgy into entertainment complete with clown suits, balloons, and so on. I also include here things like celebrating a Mass on the theme of "new life" at Easter, instead of directly allowing the Bible and the liturgy to introduce children to the resurrection; or using an e. e. cummings poem like "I thank you, God, for most this amazing day" instead of singing an Easter carol which presents the source of our amazement in all its concreteness. Here, too, I wonder if, behind the concern for children (which is its main excuse) such adaptations are really for the sake of the adults. Who, after all, is this "Sunday Morning at the Improv" addressed to? As with the sermons, I suspect that this is very often a way of getting at the adults. The Mass is being used, the children are being used to communicate indirectly to the adults. Often it is a way of treating the adults as children. Frequently, too, it is a concession to our enormous cultural appetite for entertainment.

Children as Members of the Assembly

If focusing on children in the ways just described is, in my view, not desirable, then how do we see children in the assembly of the church? I believe that children need liturgical initiation and that they have a right to a proclamation of the word that truly addresses them. There may well be a place, therefore, for children's liturgies of the word, and for ritual celebrations of prayer outside the Sunday liturgy. But our focus is the Sunday liturgy of the parish, and here I believe we should make no accommodation to our children. Rather than bring the liturgy down to their level, I believe them better served by being surrounded by adult Christians celebrating an adult faith in an adult way. Why do I hold this conviction?

First, because I believe children have a natural affinity to God that is not really fostered by much of what we do "for the sake of the children." A number of authors[25] writing on the religious life of childhood and especially early childhood confirm insights gleaned from my limited experience with my own children. These would include the power of the symbols of light and darkness; the sense that all things ultimately derive from God and have to do with God; the sense of God's omnipresence and of God's active interest in the life of the world. Children have an innate, connatural sense of the greatness of God and of God's boundlessness. As one of my boys suddenly put it at the end of grace before breakfast: "God is bigger than Jesus, God is bigger than the sun, God is bigger than the moon, God is bigger than everything." Children also have a sense that God is a world somehow more real than the one we see and touch; fascinating, therefore, but also a little intimidating; offering the possibility of intimacy, certainly, but always to be looked up to, never to be brought down to our level.

The truth is that the children live in God and God in them. They are baptized in water and the Spirit and made members of the household of faith. They are no less members of Christ's body than we are, even if we do bar them from the anointing of confirmation and from taking their place with the rest of the family at the table of the Lord. As my daughter once put it at about the age of four: "Daddy, when we go to church, you are no longer my daddy; you are my brother." There is a radical equality in the Christian community which is betrayed—and the children know it—when we condescend to them.

It is my conviction that early childhood is the natural time for children to enjoy a lively, engaged relationship with God. It is the time when their curiosity about the world, their love of stories and their even greater love of explanations, makes them eager to learn of the mystery of God that underlies and sustains the mystery of their existence. Indeed, they seem to draw on deep contemplative wells of their own. As he was being driven to kindergarten one morning, my youngest child suddenly broke the silence and said: "Only God knows where the middle of anything is." Most parents seem to have similar experiences, so it is easy to see why the ancients thought children still to be partly living in the other world. Somehow, as we grow up and grow more sophisticated, such early openness yields to the constraints of obligation, to doctrinal literalism and religious formalism, and God becomes one more thing in an overcrowded world. And so it remains, until sickness or age undermines the edifice of knowledge and habit that we have built around our lives and reduces us once again to the status of children, and to the mixture of simplicity, dependence and poverty that allows God to become God once again for us.

This is not to say that we have nothing to teach our children and that they have no need of initiation into the Christian life. On the contrary, they need to learn from us the names of God, and the stories that make sense of God and the rituals whereby we respond to God. But here's the rub. For better or worse, the ways in which we name God and imagine God and act toward God are passed on consciously or unconsciously to our children and serve to become the filters of the children's own experience. Thus, what should help children's relationship with God can all too often merely obstruct it; in trying to introduce them to God—as we like to think, on their own level—we may actually be rendering God ridiculous and inhibiting their spontaneity. As David Heller rather sadly remarked, reflecting on his study of grade school children: Children "desire a more direct encounter or experience with their God. They seem, however, to feel that such encounters are forbidden."[26]

That is why we may sometimes have to work for the conversion of children, the deliberate effort to help them recover from the harmful influences to which they have been exposed.[27] In "Landscaping the Imagination," Paul Philibert draws attention to the enormous power of the media to invade and capture the imagination of the young. Robert Duggan and Maureen Kelly, in *The Christian Initiation of Children*, write of the need to help children discriminate among what they see and hear, to help them become critics of the media, so that they recognize a "come-on" for what it is and realize that a TV story can really be a form of salesmanship. We need, in

Paul Philibert's thinking, to enter actively into the struggle to preserve and protect the religious imagination of our children, not least from our own distortions. We have actively to counteract the images and values that flood in upon them from all directions. Duggan and Kelly urge us to be aware of the competition and to work for the conversion of our children, that is to say, for the significant recentering of their images of value and power.[28] This cannot be left to the catechism lesson, nor even to the home. We need to be a community where alternative images, values and stories to live by are available. We need to be a community that actively embodies such stories, images and values, and thus provides a credible structure within which children can live and act out these Christian values. We need to do this not only as families, but as local churches; not only in the home, but in and around the church.[29]

Conclusions

While the whole of the Christian life cannot be reduced to liturgy, it is nonetheless in the liturgical assembly that we are seen for what we are. We need to communicate in the manner, style, atmosphere and ethos of our coming together that we have a profound reverence for God and profound gratitude for all the wonders of God. Saying and singing it is not enough: It comes across in the way we genuflect, in how we listen to the gospel, in the way we hold ourselves.

That is why attempts to bring God down to our level, to make the liturgy a kind of playtime, to introduce jokes and quips and applause into the liturgy "for the sake of the children" is actually a mistake. Are adults who do this sort of thing reacting against their own religious upbringing? Just as surely as the old catechism and the threats of divine punishment represented the infliction upon children of the fears and anxieties of adult religion, so making God a sugar daddy and the liturgy a weekly religious entertainment is more a statement of who and where we are as late twentieth-century adult Catholics than it is a healthy move to bring God to the children or the children to God.

If children belong in the assembly and have the right to be present at an adult liturgy, what of the young and the restless? What of the squealing infant, or the siblings pursuing their rivalry under the pew? Augustine thought he saw in such behavior the evidence of the *fomes peccati*, the after-effects of original sin. I prefer the view put forward by a Dominican preacher I heard some years ago. It was a liturgy for the public anointing of the sick, and he began by remarking that, with all the wheelchairs and canes and blankets, the place looked more like a hospital than a church. Quite right, he said, and so it should: It should look like a hospital. And it should look like a shelter for the homeless, a home for the aged, an asylum for the handicapped, a reception center for minorities and a nursery for children. An assembly of neatly turned out middle-class folks in suits and bonnets, all arranged motionless in parallel pews, is not yet an adequate sign of the assembly that God is gathering to himself. Such an assembly, as Flannery O'Connor knew, is untidy, slightly scandalous, rather bedraggled, but together.

The word is "together." The Acts of the Apostles says repeatedly that "they met together in one place." The tautology is emphatic: *together* in one place. And this is where the question arises of the kind of liturgy we are to celebrate. If not balloons and children's dramatizations, what? What we need is a liturgy that speaks to the child in each of us. Note that I say to the child in each of us: to the child as described; the child as captivated by the symbols of light and darkness; the child for whom all things ultimately derive from God and have to do with God; the child for whom God is omnipresent and actively interested in the life of the world. We need a liturgy that bespeaks God's immensity and incomprehensibility as experienced by children; a liturgy in which God is a world somehow more real than the one we see and touch; fascinating, if intimidating; offering the possibility of intimacy, certainly, but always to be looked up to, never to be brought down to our level.

Much of contemporary liturgy moves in other directions: toward dusty formalism, soupy sentimentalism, plain moralizing and/or religious entertainment. In short, most Catholic liturgy today is painfully banal. Paradoxically, our most urgent need is not for more creativity but for greater discipline; not for novelty but for repetition; not for complexity but for simplicity; not for bringing God down to our level, but for revealing the God we can look up to.

Hence the importance of the children in the church. It is not that we need childish liturgies; they seem to answer more the "needs" of the adults than those of children. We need liturgies that reflect the proclivities of children: liturgies that respect God's majesty; liturgies that are sufficiently self-sustaining that they do not require all of us to be wholly attentive all of the time; liturgies that are repetitive to the point where the chants and actions can be learned by heart, becoming so deeply familiar that they begin to color and shape the landscape of our religious imagination. Solemnity, dignity, seriousness, openness: These are the qualities of good liturgy and none of them is alien to young children. Which perhaps was why Jesus, in a solemn moment, sat down, summoned the twelve in what could be considered the first plenary assembly of the apostolic college—and set a child in their midst. "And taking the child in his arms he said to them, 'Whoever receives one such child in my name, receives me; and whoever receives me, receives not me but him who sent me.'" What stronger affirmation of the place of children in the assembly could one possibly demand?

Notes

1. This is a topic more studied in the 1960s than today. Some key references would include: Alex Blochinger, *The Modern Parish Community* (London: Chapman, 1965); Conference St. Serge, *L'assemblée liturgique et les différentes rôles dan l'assemblée* (Rome: Edizioni liturgichi, 1977), English translation: *Roles in the Liturgical Assembly* (New York: Pueblo, 1981); Yves Congar, "L'ecclesia ou communauté chrétienne, sujet integral de l'action liturgique," in Congar and J-P. Jossua, *La liturgie après Vatican II* (Paris: Cerf, 1967), 241–87; Yves Congar, "Reflexions et récherches actuelles sur l'assemblée liturgique," *La Maison-Dieu* 115 (1973): 7–29; Thierry Maertens, *Assembly for Christ* (London: Darton, Longman and Todd, 1970); Karl Rahner, "The Presence of the Lord in the Christian Community at Worship," in his *Theological Investigations*, vol. 10 (Baltimore: Helicon Press, 1973), 71–83; Johannes Wagner, ed., *The Church Worships* [same as *Concilium*, v. 12] (Glen Rock NJ: Paulist, 1966).

2. The most comprehensive study is that of Maria-Regina Botterman, *Die Beteiligung des Kindes an der Liturgie von den Anfängen der Kirche bis Heute* (Frankfurt/Bonn: P. Lang, 1982).

3. The third-century Apostolic Tradition of Hippolytus indicates that after the communal supper with its solemn service of light, "they shall rise and pray and the boys and the virgins shall sing psalms"; ed. G. J. Cuming, *Hippolytus: A Text for Students* (Bramcote Notts: Grove, 1976), 24. The alternation of psalms by boys and virgins is mentioned again in the

late fourth-century *Testament of the Lord*, 2:4; ed. Rahmani, 167. In the account of her pilgrimage (ca. 386), Egeria recounts that at the end of vespers each evening, the boys *(pisinni)* sang the Kyries in response to the intercessions voiced by the deacon; J. Wilkinson, *Egeria's Travels*, 24:5 (London: SPCK, 1971), 124. According to the *Testament of the Lord*, 2:11, the whole people responded to the verses of psalms sung by the boys at the "Lighting of the lamps," ed. Rahmani, 135. Other evidence can be found in J. Quasten, "The Development of Boys' Singing in the Christian Liturgy: *Lectores infantuli*," in *Music and Worship in Pagan and Christian Antiquity* (Washington: Pastoral Press, 1983), 87–92.

[4] The best known of these were at the Lateran and St. Peter's.

[5] The *schola cantorum lectorumque* (choir-school of lectors and cantors) was already in place when Gregory the Great (590–604) established daily (?) Masses at the "four apostolic basilicas and appointed the necessary chanters;" see S. J. P. Van Dijk, "Gregory the Great, Founder of the Urban Schola Cantorum," *Ephemerides Liturgique* 77 (1963): 335–56.

[6] For the ordination of lectors see *Ordo Romanus XXXV*:1–16 in M. Andrieu, ed., *Les Ordines romani du haut moyen âge* 4, Spicilegium Lovaniense 28 (Louvain, 1956), 33–5; M. Andrieu, "Les ordres mineurs dans l'ancien rit romain," in *Revue des Sciences religieuses* 5 (1925):232–74. The Gallican ordination of lectors and the appointment of psalmists is mentioned in the *Statua Ecclesiae Antiqua* (ca. 476–485). Other early evidence is listed in C. Vogel, *Medieval Liturgy: Introduction to the Sources* (Washington: Pastoral Press, 1986), 175–76.

[7] The Rule of St. Benedict (480–543) includes directions for the reception of youngsters or "oblates" (chapter 59). This rule was used in almost every monastery of Europe from about 817 until the thirteenth century.

[8] K. Edwards, *The English Secular Cathedrals in the Middle Ages* (Manchester: Manchester University Press, 2nd edition 1967), 311.

[9] Charles Pietri has shown that there were two "tracks" of ecclesiastical advancement (*cursus honorum*) in the Rome of late antiquity—one for the presbyterate and the other for the diaconate—both of which began in the *schola cantorum lectorumque*. To become a presbyter, one would be ordained an acolyte, and after a prescribed time might be ordained presbyter of one of the Roman *tituli* or of some suburban church. In the other cursus, one could be named subdeacon and if lucky, one of the regional subdeacons. The next step would be to the college of seven deacons from which the archdeacon was chosen. The bishop could be chosen from either *cursus*, and it was not until the eighth century that all the orders were considered essential steps to the episcopacy; *Roma Christiana: Récherches sur l'Église de Rome, Son organisation, sa politique, son idéologie de Militiade à Sixte III (311–440)*, Bibliothéque des École francaises d'Athènes et de Rome, 224 (Rome: Fârnèse, 1976), 690–696. See also M. Andrieu, "La carrière ecclésiastique des papes et les documents liturgiques du moyen âge," *Revue des Sciences religieuses* 21 (1947): 90–120 and his article cited above in note 6.

[10] L. Duchesne, ed., *Le Liber Pontificalis*, I (Paris: Bocard, 1886; reprint 1955), 371: After coming from Sicily during the pontificate of Adeodatus (672–76), Sergius I (687–701) was "numbered among the Roman clergy and, because he was eager and clever *in officio cantilenae*, he was handed over to the prior of the schola *pro doctrina*." His namesake, Sergius II (844–47), entered the schola when he was orphaned at age 12, and when he became pope, renovated its headquarters—the *orphanotropheum*—up the Via Merulana from the Lateran; see *Liber Pontificalis*, II (Paris: Bocard, 1890; reprint 1955), 92.

[11] See Botterman, 58.

[12] See T. Wiedemann, *Adults and Children in the Roman Empire* (New Haven: Yale University Press, 1989), 176ff.

[13] At least as late as the third century; see Wiedemann, 182.

[14] See Wiedemann, 185. While infant mortality rates are notoriously difficult to establish with any reliability, Wiedemann considers a 39% infant mortality rate about right, with 49% of children reaching the age of five and about 40% reaching 20. Generally, life expectancy was about 20–25 years in the late Roman republic. Parents would have a 50/50 chance of any child reaching the age of 10, while two out of five might reach adulthood.

[15] Wiedemann, 186.

[16] See, for example, the *Epistle to Diognetus,* 5, in M. Staniforth, translator and editor, *Early Christian Writings* (Baltimore: Penguin, 1968; reprinted 1975), [171–85] 176–77, and in other collections of writings from that time.

[17] And in Judaism as well: It was the boy, Daniel, who refused to have anything to do with Susanna's unjust sentence of death (Daniel 13: 47ff).

[18] "No drunken orgies, no promiscuity or licentiousness, and no wrangling or jealousy, but rather put on the Lord Jesus Christ and forget about satisfying your bodies with all their cravings." *The Confessions of St. Augustine*, Book 8, chapter 12, 29–30.

[19] For a first-hand account of such proceedings in Stanbrook Abbey in England at the turn of this century, see M. H. Hastings, "Christmas at Stanbrook Abbey," *Downside Review* 108 (1990): 62–65.

[20] James F. Hopewell, *Congregation: Stories and Structures,* (Fortress: Philadelphia, 1987), 7.

[21] Hopewell, 8.

[22] Editor's note: "Sanctuary" is used by many Christians for "the worship space," i.e., what Roman Catholics call "the church." The Catholic "sanctuary" is often termed the "chancel."

[23] Hopewell, 8.

[24] The term "congregations" is used advisedly, since different congregations in the same parish can have quite different identities, depending in part on their attitude toward children.

[25] See among others: Sofia Cavalletti, *The Religious Potential of the Child* (Chicago: Liturgy Training Publications, 1992); Edwin Robinson, *The Original Vision. A Study of the Religious Experience of Childhood* (New York: Seabury, 1983); David Heller, *The Children's God* (Chicago: University of Chicago Press, 1986); Robert Coles, *The Spiritual Life of Children* (Boston: Houghton Mifflin, 1990).

[26] Heller, 134.

[27] Maria Montessori used this term in a broadly pedagogical sense in the 1930s. See *The Mass Explained to Children* (London: Sheed and Ward, 1932) and *The Mass Explained to Boys and Girls* (London/New York: Sheed and Ward; New York/Chicago: Sadlier, 1934).

[28] Robert B. Duggan and Maureen A. Kelly, *The Christian Initiation of Children: Hope for the Future* (Mahwah NJ: Paulist, 1991), esp. 89–111.

[29] See Craig Dykstra, "The Formative Power of the Congregation," in *Religious Education* 82:4 (1987): 530–546.

Gertrud Mueller Nelson

Adults and Children in the Art of Celebration

When our youngest child was about four, she fashioned banners of whatever scraps she could find in my sewing basket and could glue to the end of a pole. She called these her "precessions." "We need a precession," she would say, leaning over her work "so that God can come down and dance with us." Then raising her banner into the wind, slowly, she would begin to dance.

That's all it takes when you are four: some strips of cloth, a stick, a wad of tape, and God is your partner in a dance. In our innocence, God isn't distant. In innocence we dance with God and are God's equal partner.

The Kingdom of Heaven

But as we grow, it seems to be our fate to grow more distant in our easy relationship with God. And we are, all of us, from those days onward, ever trying to reconnect with heaven and with an experience of God we once had and may now only "remember" in fleeting moments that masquerade as nostalgia or longing.

That longing—to bring heaven and earth to the same place—is in fact our greatest desire, whether we are conscious of it or not. It is also our singular calling. To bring together the great opposites, heaven and earth, God and humanity, Spirit and matter, is to participate in the mystery of the incarnation—a mystery that happens over and over again wherever grace supports it and we allow it.

This marriage is at once the most difficult thing we can ever participate in, because we are asked to help heal a great split between opposites, and it is also the most simple and rewarding experience we may ever have. It is the mystery we long to experience but fear is out of our reach; and it is a mystery so astonishingly close and easily possible that we often fail to recognize it. For the kingdom of God is at hand.

The kingdom of God is actually underfoot—yet this seems to be the place we least often look for our religious connection to God. And often, to scan the heavens and try to find God "out there" means we are already looking in the wrong direction. When we look to what has been forgotten (or "at hand" and taken for granted, to what has been shunned or despised or misunderstood), we come to know that we have already found God's dwelling place. For today the "ascent of Mount Carmel" must be, in fact, a descent. The more down to earth we are, and the more human we are, the more likely we are to taste something of God.

The incarnation is that breakthrough by which we come to know God's passionate love and union with humankind as the end of all divisions. The incarnation makes holy all materiality and bodiliness and all the things of this earth. This holiness of every little scrap—the strips of discarded cloth in the basket—as conduit or container of God-with-us is something that any child knows. Thus, when I speak of children I refer not only to young people, but include (and this with all sincerity and urgency) the child within each of us, that innocent one that Jesus said we must become again before we can enter the kingdom of heaven, before we can taste of the transcendent kingdom "on earth as it is in heaven."

Prayer and play and the art of living are not values we develop to impose on those shorter than we are. Rather, do we not discover more often than not, that the principles of prayer and play and the art of living life with passion and wonder are things which children teach us? They already know the holy moments. For them, the "religious experience" of the kingdom of heaven is all part of a day's work.

Children are born into our lives already the residents of the garden of Eden. They don't yet know the difference between good and evil. They are pleased with their bodies and unashamed of their nakedness. And until their "taste of knowledge"—or our culture—ends for them this season of wonder, they walk and talk with God.

It is, then, our holy duty as parents and teachers, not to chase our children from that garden of innocence too soon, nor insist on their participation in our cultural aberrations before their time, before they have tasted and absorbed in their own good time the fullness of God's goodness and nurture in every aspect of their sensorial development. Those early and deeply formative experiences of God-with-us are formed in us, for better or for worse, through our earliest experiences with our parents.

Infant Religious Experience

Infant religious experiences are real and are no less worthy than the religious experiences of the disciplined mystic. In fact, they are wonderfully, delightfully similar. To cry for milk and then be warmly gathered up to nurse at the breast and be satisfied is a religious experience: It is to be nourished in the "land flowing with milk and honey." In that primal experience we come to learn that God knows our need and fills it and floods us with unqualified love.

To be two years old and have a bowel movement is a highly charged, autonomous, satisfying and creative act! "See this thing I have made," the child seems to say, "and with no one's help." "I made it all alone. I made it out of nothing. Like God, I am a creator, and I, too, see that it is good."

One of our children was so delighted in her productions that she called in any available family member—and even any guest—for a viewing. Pointing to her little potty she'd say with boundless joy, "See! Today I made a camel!" Or on another day, with equal surprise, "I made a buffalo!" or "I made a seal!" One time at the table she passed gas and looked about with surprise and announced, "Oh! Buffalo burped!"

At ages two and three one learns that to co-create with God is a wonderful act, but not synonymous with being God. In fact, the trick is to offer one's gift on the right altar and watch all the minor powers smile.

We teach our children that every good thing has its time and its place. Misplaced, these good things do not lose their intrinsic goodness, but perhaps they become uncomfortable and impractical, impolite or inappropriate. Sometimes we cringe when our youngsters tell potty stories to one another (which they inevitably do) as though it were some reflection on us. As adults, we think we have outgrown such infantile fascinations, but the power of these basic and early religious experiences are still (and often) evident in our so-called "adult" language. Often, incantations to God and excrement explode in the same breath when adults are caught off guard. Out of the unconscious, we still hear the power of childhood wonders and may as well take the cue and learn to honor those experiences on the right level and at the appropriate developmental stage. The only difference between the early mystical experiences of the infant and the recognition of mystery by the mystic is the matter of consciousness.

Religious Experience of the Mystic

Dame Julian of Norwich said:

> Food is shut in within our bodies as in a very beautiful purse. When necessity calls, the purse opens and then shuts again, in the most fitting way. And it is God who does this. God does not despise creation, nor does God disdain to serve us in the simplest function that belongs to our bodies in nature. . . . As the body is clothed in cloth and the muscles in the skin and the bones in the muscles and the heart in the chest, so are we, body and soul, clothed in the goodness of God and enclosed.[1]

As so-called adults, we seem to spend a very long time between our mystical experiences in infancy and childhood and the completion of the circle in holy wisdom and mystical simplicity at the end of life. Because in our culture we have so little regard for early religious experiences, and because we spend so many years trying to remove ourselves from a direct experience of what is natural and nature itself, we often deprive ourselves of that experience of God, which can be caught only through the simplicity of matter.

It is our own "adult" distortions that remove us from God and make the transcendent distant, difficult and beyond our reach. But when ordinary matter is shot through and shining with mystery, we see beyond it the ineffable mystery which is God.

The Role of the Adult

To work with children, then, is our privilege. If we give them reason to trust us, children can reconnect us to the God who became distant because of our complexities. Children will give us all the ingredients necessary for making a moment holy; and often, because we are the adults nearby, these ingredients are for us to interpret and refine with reverence and *return them to the children with form and worth.* ("Worship" means "to impart worth.")

It is our job as adults to give back reverence and worth. It is not to overvalue or to undervalue an experience or a creation, but to give it the right worth. (The buffalo, while a holy production, was never bronzed to be put on a shelf! Not every scrawl dashed off by a child is meant to be posted for display on the refrigerator door.) Rather, process must be given its worth—given equal value—in this world that overvalues product.

More often than not, the art of liturgical action is the art of living a process—of healing and making conscious our humanness. In liturgy, art is less often the thing in itself which we make and then think we must keep. The Navajo Indian knows that the sandpainting is the art of healing, not of painting, for which the unquestionably beautiful sandpainting serves only until it is wiped away again and swept into the winds. In sacramental action, the bread is broken, shared and consumed. The precious incense is burned away. The ashes are washed off at the end of Ash Wednesday. The wreath dries up. The Christmas tree is dragged away again. The Easter egg is cracked and eaten. The baptismal candle burns down and consumes itself. But each of these ordinary and natural things has engaged us physically and emotionally in a truth about the mysteries of our human nature and the story of our salvation. Each serves a purpose: to hold, for a time, a meaning and to point beyond itself to mystery.

Ultimately, every human developmental cycle is a process worthy of form and ritual. In ritual, we give worth—worth-ship. Ritual is the formal and physical expression of what is holy. It is the art of living the mystery of God through the ordinary tasks and transitions that make us fully human.

Seasons and Cycles

Carl Jung, addressing a group of Episcopalian bishops, once said that the Catholic Church had everything one needed to live wholly and to be made whole. In its liturgical action the Church reaches beyond the intellectual and speaks to the core and mystery of our common human experience where it will heal and unify, validate and affirm all that we know in our deepest human sphere. The liturgical year and the sacraments and sacramentals of the Church celebrate and validate the fundamental human experiences of birthing and living, of loving and failing, of healing and reconciling, of dying and being reborn—and all of this in the life of Jesus the Christ.

In feasting and fasting together with our fully human passions and pathos we become a people united and transfigured by God whose disclosure in time gave us the ultimate feast beyond all time. In truth, it is only in the very humanness of our common experience that we can be brought together with the divine. To celebrate the seasons of the church year, to celebrate all aspects of life in sacrament and sacramentals—these are invitations to live our human life with passion and consciousness.

The elements of these rituals and celebrations are only the earthy and readily available things of this world: everything that appeals to what is most simple in us and what is, therefore, most powerful—bread and wine, water and fire, earth and ashes and oil, tears, seeds and songs, flowers and branches, bodies and babies, the smells of burning resin and aromatic ointments, the sound of instruments and bells and voices, the telling of stories, the rhythms of nature—its mornings and evenings, its dark days and light days, its lying fallow, its springtimes and harvests. The liturgical year gives shape to the rhythms of our souls, to the seasons of darkness and light, death and life, that we know in our hearts.

Human Developmental Cycles

What we do, then, with our children need not be very different from what we need to do for ourselves. We must be aware of all our developmental cycles. We talk of the ages and stages of babies—of potty training and of "the terrible twos." But do we know their worth and value? Do we know them as sacramental? Does not "terrible twos" say that this is a stage we dread and perhaps don't understand, or value as a marvelous first battle for autonomy and identity and separation from the former merging that made mother and baby all of a piece?

Do we know that whatever we didn't resolve during the terrible twos will be served up again for us in adolescence—another time which we've come to dread and devalue and condemn and misunderstand?

Up the road, do we know as holy and worthy that which we've come to call the "mid-life crisis," another chance to repair what we left undone during the terrible twos and during our adolescence? Birth and death and rebirth —all are grace-filled cycles on the way to our ultimate transformation.

We need to look at how we love and give birth, how we buy our first house, how we fight and make up, how we deal with sickness and taxes, with pain and loss and death, with reconciliation, with healing, transformation, rebirth. All these moments can be sacramental.

Cycle of the Day

Even in the cycle of the day, we see in microcosm the whole cycle of birth and life and death and rebirth. It is a cycle fraught with transitions, moments when we want to regress to a place we knew earlier that worked for us, moments when we unconsciously try to avoid looking into the future, for the future seems often a frightening unknown.

We could say that to wake in the morning is to be born to a new day, wanting at the same time to go back to sleep—just five minutes longer. To shower and dress is to be baptized, to be cleansed of darkness and refreshed with new life—and still we may dread another day at work.

To make this moment sacramental is to name and bless the transition we are undertaking. It can be a moment to reflect on our baptism as we name ourselves again; that is, renew our identity and purpose as we put on the garment appropriate to our task and calling. It is holy baptism that seals and ratifies this everyday experience of renewal and initiation, of calling and commitment. Baptism returns purpose to all those small or great ways we experience such moments of rebirth in our lives.

We eat breakfast and it is a time for communion with our family, nourishment for the road and the nourishment of one another as we go forth to love and serve the Lord. We leave the shelter of our house to enter the greater community. We are called to make peace. We are called to be reconciled. We seek healing and offer healing out of our own woundedness.

We co-create with God. We do what we can to bring about the kingdom on earth as it is in heaven. We return home to touch base again, to regroup, to receive and to give, to share and to retreat, to nourish and to be nourished. To assess the day. To take responsibility. To make resolutions. To amend. To bring the day to a close. To die a little death in sleep.

Children know that these little cycles are fraught with expectation and danger. They will bring you the ingredients to make of this day a cycle of growth and meaning. They can drive you to distraction with all their little quirks and habits and requirements—unless, of course, you understand these quirks, reorder them and give them back in form and order, imbued with right value and worth.

A small child at bedtime will want this toothpaste and not that one, a bath and not a shower, this truck in bed with him and not the teddy bear, this story—and woe to you if you skip or change some words—and not that one. The hall door open "this far." The closet door closed. The light off in the kitchen and on in the bathroom.

The adult, aware that this is all the stuff of ritual for the close of a day and the entry into the "close and holy darkness," will reorder these ingredients and give them back with worth and meaning. Washing, brushing, flossing—the practical things get done. Stories are told and stories are heard and these will engage a range of feelings and spend them. One names the fears and doesn't brush them aside as though the inner world of the soul were not a real world. We close the day with a certain holy routine that the child can always count on—one that brings closure, peace and comfort. A prayer. A blessing, perhaps, with the Easter water that named us and gives us a place in this world and in God's great scheme of things. And a final "Good night—God bless."

Cycle of the Week

The week has the same rhythm. Each day needs to have its own flavor and character—its own tasks. True to tradition, the church offers a day to engage our own darkness and death and a day to celebrate new life and new beginnings. By making every day the same, we deprive ourselves of engaging the rhythms of life. And the rhythms of life left unrecognized will take over, and we become vulnerable, for instance, to having a bad day, any and every day.

In the tradition of the church, Friday was a day of atonement and reconciliation. Christians were invited to engage in the passion and death of Jesus and to engage all those areas in their own lives that needed to die. It was a ritual "bad day." It was a day (if we didn't reduce it to magic and superstitions) which we took to ourselves with consciousness. Imagine we should take Friday back and only after we make it a mini-Good Friday through fasting and abstinence, special prayer, and acts of reconciliation and kindness, dare we sigh: "Thank God it's Friday"—and bring the work week to its end.

That sigh actually indicates myriad unspoken hopes and longings expressed in a tumble of expectations: We want to have a good time this weekend, but we also expect to get certain things done. We intend to get caught up, and we expect to have fun. We intend to spend time with the family, and we expect to find some time for ourselves. We expect to relax, and we expect to be uplifted in an hour at our parish. In that sigh we express a wish that the coming weekend will actually lift us out of our routine and boredom and give us meaning and re-creation and, indeed, a taste of that God we just thanked for giving us Friday. We actually want a religious experience. This experience can't be had by pulling into the spiritual filling station for a week's fix. Sitting back in the pew, we dare someone to give us a religious experience. With all these vague expectations, it is no wonder that by four o'clock on Sunday afternoon the world seems grey and Monday promises to be blue.

If, however, we have come to learn that we are the church and that we bring ourselves and our week's experiences to be ratified and transformed in our participation in Sunday's liturgical experience, we will know the need to prepare and shape our weekend. No child, old or young, ripped out of bed and coming to the gospel message cold, gets much out of it. If we want, all of us, to be present for word and feast, then we will benefit by coming prepared. Reinstating Sunday observance does not take superhuman spiritual exercises. It means undertaking to do a few small things, consciously. Imagine the family that takes a few minutes to read and discuss the gospel story before coming to the parish church. Imagine, as a parent, telling the gospel as a story in a way that the children can understand—and then reading it in the formal words of scripture so that we can watch out for these words and recognize them the next day when they are proclaimed during the eucharistic celebration.

We can do certain simple things to make this day different from all other days. We reinstate an old custom and dress in our Sunday best for church because Sunday clothes are a reminder of our baptismal garments. We prepare a meal to be eaten together with family and/or friends at the dining room table with the good dishes and a table cloth. Later, changed into more casual clothes, we re-create. We experience this world and know that it is good.

But when Sunday is reduced to changing the oil, doing the bills, getting caught up with the laundry, finally sitting down to homework, or plying the shopping malls, we deprive ourselves of an experience of Sunday as the eighth day—the day set apart and over and above time—a time out of time. We will not recognize our own change on that final day of rebirth and resurrection because we were busy catching up on the chores.

Every Sunday is a part of the great wheel in the church year and expresses some aspect of the year and of the developmental cycles of our own becoming. Each of these seasons has its own theme, its own joys and pains, its own requirements, its own readings, psalms, hymns, songs and celebrations. It also has its own games, recipes, artistic expressions, folk customs and family/parish fasts or festivities.

Gertrud Mueller Nelson

Cycle of the Church Year

The feasts and seasons of the church year correspond to our personal cycles of development. In Advent we celebrate God's love for us, a love so passionate that God had to become one of us; heaven and earth become one. In the mystery of Advent we all become pregnant and enter a period of anticipation and waiting, waiting for the birth of the God-man and for his return on the final day. The archetype of waiting in Advent is an experience that connects us to every sort of waiting and pregnancy that our personal lives might ever know, from waiting for the elevator, for the x-rays to come back, for someone to understand us, to waiting for a healing of the split that keeps matter and spirit separate and disconnected on every level.

At Christmas we celebrate the coming of the Savior and new hope. Because of the incarnation (literally the flesh-taking), all matter becomes holy. The human body, the barn, the smell of beasts, the company of peasant-folk—all this was, for heaven, the perfect setting for the birth of God-with-us. In fact, such a setting reminds us that God is found in exactly the place where we have come least to expect our salvation—there between the straw and the manure piles of our human experience.

Lent offers us the forms, the readings and disciplines to suffer and to die to our false selves. Through the Lord's own passion we learn to understand the sufferings that weave in and out of our own daily lives, the necessary crosses that are mysteriously required for our glorious rebirth in baptism and our transformation in the Easter mysteries.

From the feasts and mysteries of the church year we draw the sort of nourishment and meaning that is the only antidote I know to the poisons of our consumer culture. In celebrating these feasts and fasts we are given the forms we need to become healed and whole; and we have the sacramentals, all the customs and ceremonies of domestic life, to make every human experience whole. In the rites of our liturgy the right worth (worship) is given to both spirit and matter. Through the celebration of the year's sacred mysteries, we will find new meaning in what is otherwise routine or a stiffened "custom." We will find it a worthy container for what we already realize in our hearts.

This means that in the parish community, in the school and in the family, if we are honest about living the cycle of the church calendar, we will come to know and touch and be touched by the mysteries of each season. We will live our lives artfully and create from of simple actions, transitions and experiences that work of art which is healing grace, transformation and a taste of the divine.

A Hopi Rite of Passage

To be adult in the true sense of the word—one who is committed to the service of the children in our families, communities and worshiping communities, and who is yet childlike in the way that Jesus said was required of us to experience the kingdom—is a development profoundly to be wished for. It is a spiritual process as much as it is a social or psychological one. It is also a long, drawn-out and often failed process in our modern society.

A ritual performed by Southwest Indians in the service of that seemingly tricky process is a good example of what I wish to convey here. (So often it helps to look to another culture's religious behaviors in order to understand or ratify our own processes.) This ritual tells of the relationship of adults to children in the sacred mysteries of transition, growth and transformation.[2] It tells something about the importance of ritual, "sacred play" and liturgical action for all of us, adult or child. And it leaves to the grace of God, to human will and to individual commitment the actual art of becoming an adult.

On the feast of the Kachinas, Hopi children gather in the great earthen kiva as they have always done, year after year. They have descended through a hole at the top of this domed, sacred space to await the dancing gods as they come down from the sacred mountains. They listen for the sound of the Kachinas approaching with their calling and chanting. The gods come nearer and nearer and finally enter through the hole at the top of the kiva and descend. They come to frighten the children with their masks, to dance their dances, to tell their ancient stories and to give their gifts and blessings.

Then one day the children, who have now become adolescents, gather again in the kiva to await the gods—just as they have done every year of their lives. Again, chanting and calling and bearing their gifts, the Kachinas arrive and descend into their midst. But this time the gods are not dressed in their special masks and robes. The young people see for the first time that the Kachinas are the community elders and their fathers and uncles and older brothers! Without explanation, the ceremony proceeds as it always has. Then the Kachinas ascend again and disperse.

The revelation shatters a naive faith. Thus "disenchanted," the adolescents are wordlessly given a profound religious choice. They can be disappointed and distressed at having been misled all these years and regret their lost innocence and abandon their Kachinas as childish. Or they can see this as a ritual invitation into adulthood. This time, at the close of the ceremony, for them to ascend and leave through the hole at the top of the earthen kiva will mean a transformation—a rebirth out of this Mother Earth and into their community—now, as adults. It may dawn on them that to follow the elders out is to join with those who know their calling is to participate in the godly work of the Kachinas. To be an adult is to tell the ancient stories, to give the gifts, to make human and incarnational this work of the gods.

"Disenchantment" can unfortunately be the state we linger in as grown people, always in mourning, bitter and disappointed over our lost innocence, always hoping that "the church" will provide us the religious experience our soul longs for, always the children who refuse to grow up and take our part in the work of God. On the other hand, our disenchantments and our lost innocence can be our transformation and lead to that resurrection of the spirit which invites us into the experience of mystery, of faith, of a spirituality or sacramentality which imbues all life with meaning and grace. As true adults, we participate in God's mysteries, we tell the stories, we pass on the gifts, we dance the dances and disperse the blessings. Only as adults can we become as simple and faithful as children again and do our part as conduits of God's work among us. In God's mysterious providence, God chooses to "need" us to make human and incarnational the grace and mystery of our redemption through Christ Jesus.

Notes

[1] Julian of Norwich, *Showings: The Long Text,* Chapter VI; trans. E. Colledge and J. Walsh (New York: Paulist Press, 1978), 186.

[2] John Shea, *Stories of God: An Unauthorized Biography,* (Chicago: The Thomas More Press, 1978), 32–33. Shea cites an article by Sam D. Gill, "Disenchantment," *Parabola,* Vol. 1 (Spring 1976) and includes the following quotation from Gill: "The children are taken into a *kiva* [hut] to await a *kachina* dance—a now familiar event. They hear the *Kachinas* calling as they approach the *kiva.* They witness the invitation extended from within the *kiva* for the dancing gods to enter. But to the children's amazement, the *Kachinas* enter without masks, and for the first time in their lives, the initiates discover that the *kachinas* are actually members of their own village impersonating the gods."

Linda Gaupin

Separate Liturgies of the Word with Children?

During the past several years separate liturgies of the word with children have become widespread in the United States. In some parishes the practice has become normative for the Sunday celebration of the eucharist. The Sunday eucharist is the primary ritual celebration of the Christian community. Like all public rituals, it expresses and forms the identity—the pattern of relationships—of the community.[1] The inauguration of any new practice into a ritual inevitably affects and makes a statement about these relationships. What are the implications of a separate liturgy of the word for children?

Too often in the history of the church, new liturgical practices have been introduced to meet a need or to compensate for a deficiency that was not related to the liturgy. For example, in the Middle Ages when bishops ceased to preside over most baptisms, the unity of the initiation sacraments was shattered and confirmation was performed when the bishop was available, not when called for by the church's liturgical theology. In our own time, due to the shortage of priests (a situation unrelated to the liturgy itself), Sunday celebrations led by unordained ministers are replacing Sunday Mass in some areas. Such remedies do not solve the problem at hand; at most, they enable the church to cope in some way with a changed situation. The danger is that these remedies will be accepted as permanent modifications of the tradition because no one stopped to question them or to consider alternatives.

Bearing these ideas in mind, this paper investigates the phenomenon of separate liturgies of the word within the context of four related areas: (1) the liturgy itself, (2) the Christian initiation of children who have reached catechetical age,[2] (3) ecclesial relationships and (4) the relationship between liturgy and catechesis. I will first examine and summarize the insights gained from these four areas, then demonstrate the contributions these insights make to the discussion of separate liturgies of the word with children on Sundays.

Insights

The Liturgy

Since the promulgation of the *Constitution on the Sacred Liturgy* (CSL), we have begun to retrieve the fundamental insight that liturgy is the primary formative experience of church. Among all of the activities of the church, the liturgy is the summit and source of our life, and serves as the primary formative experience that both expresses and realizes what it means to be a people of God. Consequently the goal is to foster vigorous liturgical celebrations.

Liturgical worship by nature is ritual. Laden with power to form and transform, ritual takes hold of us; we do not take hold of it. In other words, the liturgy does not achieve its purpose because of the rational ability of persons to comprehend it intellectually or to articulate its meaning. As ritual, it "works" by taking over the entire lives of the participants. Ritual activity is not primarily a cerebral exercise but an engagement of the whole person. We do learn in ritual activity, but, as Aidan Kavanagh insists, liturgy teaches and forms us experientially, nondiscursively, richly, ambiguously and elementally.[3]

We do the liturgy over and over again because the repetition of the familiar, ritual pattern—as much as its content—forms us as a community of faith. Thus, in the liturgy of the word, the ritual pattern of proclamation, response, acclamation, homily and intercession, as well as the accompanying ritual gestures and postures of processing, listening, keeping silent, sitting, standing, singing and making petition are as formative of who we are as the words themselves.

A second insight retrieved in the last 25 years is the thoroughly biblical nature of liturgy. A considerable portion of what the assembly proclaims, prays, and sings is either taken directly from scripture or is closely related to it: entrance psalm, greeting, readings, responsorial psalms, Holy, institution narrative, Lord's Prayer, Lamb of God, invitation to communion and communion psalm.

Furthermore, we have come to appreciate that the liturgy does not look back to a founding event as a moment in history but renders that event present again through its enactment.[4]

The "Christian Initiation of Children Who Have Reached Catechetical Age"

With the implementation of the Rite of Christian Initiation of Adults adapted to children of catechetical age, we have come to discover anew that young children are capable of receiving and nurturing a personal faith. They possess a marvelous capacity for embracing the living word of God in their lives. (This is not the same as a clear, rational comprehension of it.)

Many have witnessed the power of the word to capture young children when, in the "Rite of Acceptance into the Order of Catechumens," they declare in the midst of the Sunday assembly that they desire to become Christian, that they believe in Christ, and that they believe in eternal life. Then, moved by the power of the word working in their lives, they offer their bodies to be marked by the sign of Christ, the cross. And on the first Sunday of Lent in the presence of the bishop and the assembly of the local church, they respond to the proclamation of the word by coming forward to sign their name in the Book of the Elect, some printing their name publicly for the first time.

Any who have witnessed this know beyond doubt that these children, publicly responding with the whole of their young lives to the proclamation of the word, are ministers to the assembly. It is not only the assembly who ministers to them.

Ecclesial Relationships

We have also begun to appreciate the liturgical assembly as a complex and diverse reality. A so-called "normative" group for every Sunday liturgy composed of fully initiated adults of a standard age, ethnic and racial background does not exist.

Neither are there "categories" of church membership. The Christian community by its very nature is inclusive; it is a body composed of many members who possess a variety of gifts, who bring to the celebration a wide range of human experiences, who have a diversity of needs. Members are in different relationships with the church at large, so that on any given Sunday, the assembly may include catechumens, elect, baptized, fully initiated, penitents, marginalized and alienated people—and within each group, there is an age range. Each group, each age within the groups, indeed each individual brings different human experiences to the liturgy of the word and has different needs of the word.

A liturgical dismissal makes a powerful and explicit statement about relationships within the assembly. Such dismissals have long been a part of liturgical celebrations and, as Aidan Kavanagh points out, "were used in one context or another to affect every group within the liturgical assembly."[5]

Earlier in our history, catechumens were dismissed from the assembly after the liturgy of the word; only the baptized could remain to pray with the faithful, exchange the kiss of peace, and partake of the body and blood of Christ. Penitents also were dismissed (not from the assembly since they were still numbered among the baptized) to "depart" or "withdraw" to a special place in the church reserved for them. The church also dismissed energumens, "those people whom Jesus himself was at pains to aid, people whose inexplicable behavior put them beyond conventional society. They appear to be those who did not suffer from conventionally diagnosed diseases, but from disorders such as epilepsy, severe ticks and psychotic manias resulting in seemingly random alterations in behavior causing social astonishment and alarm."[6] From the fifth through tenth centuries, those who were not intending to receive communion were dismissed before the distribution of communion. Dismissal structures can be found as well in the daily offices in both cathedral and monastic settings.

In examining the content of the prayers and formulas used, Kavanagh notes that the meaning of the dismissal varied "in respect to different groups within the liturgical assembly, all of which resulted in locating differently these various groups within the liturgical celebrations."[7] This practice was not a sign of social distinctions within the liturgy, but rather a recognition of the richly diverse human condition of the assembly in relationship to baptism.

As always, the faithful are dismissed at the conclusion of the eucharistic liturgy. The liturgical dismissal of catechumens, both adults and children, at the conclusion of the liturgy of the word has been restored. We are beginning to see that liturgical dismissals make a distinction among members of the assembly with respect to baptism.

Liturgy and Catechesis

Although related to each other, liturgy and catechesis are distinct activities. Catechesis forms in the faith, liturgy celebrates faith. Catechesis leads to liturgy, and liturgy naturally results in a deepening of and a need for catechesis in our lives. Confusing these activities weakens liturgy by diverting us from its purpose; confusing these activities also detracts from the major role catechesis should play in the Christian life from womb to tomb. Thus, to collapse catechesis into liturgy is to do a major disservice to both: Liturgy is forced to bear a catechetical burden for which it was not intended; catechesis loses ground in the church.

The dialogue now taking place between liturgy and catechesis holds promise for enhancing not only our liturgical life, but our catechetical ministry as well, for it can enable us to distinguish activities that are properly liturgical from those that are catechetical. When liturgy and catechesis are properly understood as separate activities, liturgy is not expected to fulfill catechetical needs; catechesis can then assume its proper role within the church.

We can now consider the questions each of these insights raises regarding separate liturgies of the word with children, and examine some of the presuppositions, theories and expectations of this phenomenon.

Contributions to the Discussion

Liturgy

If the motivaton for providing separate liturgies of the word is to help
children better "understand" something of the life of God or the church, we
may be victims of a mindset that has predominated for several centuries.
This mentality presumes that the liturgy is a rational and cognitive experience: something to be read, instead of done; that is instructional, rather
than formative; that needs explanatory, catechetical, or scientific language,
rather than the ritual language of symbol, poetry, gesture, posture, space,
music, etc. In other words, do we hold that the proper celebration of the
liturgy depends on our rational ability to fully articulate and explain it?
Constance Tarasar points out that:

> The Orthodox church has never accepted the concept that only an adult can
> truly receive and appropriate a sacrament because of rational ability. In our
> fallen state, the ability to accept or reject the gift of God [and I would add God's
> word] is determined not by one's rational abilities, but by the degree of one's
> openness to or alienation from God. One need only to look around at the
> members of any congregation to see that there are indeed children who are
> more receptive to God's word than there are adults.[8]

Louis Weil makes the same point in a slightly different way. He asks: "Is a
person not capable of receiving God's gifts until rational understanding is
reached? If so, why do we baptize infants?"[9]

What do we expect of the liturgy of the word for children (and adults,
for that matter)? Is it rational comprehension at this moment? The *Introduction* to the Lectionary for Mass states:

> In the celebration of the liturgy the word of God is not voiced in only one way,
> nor does it always stir the hearts of the hearers with the same power. Always,
> however, Christ is present in his word; as he carries out the mystery of salva-
> tion, he sanctifies us and offers the Father perfect worship. . . . That word
> constantly proclaimed in the liturgy is always, then, a living, active word
> through the power of the Holy Spirit. It expresses the Father's love that never
> fails in its effectiveness toward us.[10]

Our belief that the word of God in liturgical celebration is indeed a
living, active word through the power of the Holy Spirit calls us to trust that

L i n d a   G a u p i n

this living word embraces all who are present in the liturgical assembly. It requires that we believe that the living word of God cannot be confined or contained, that it is not limited by one's rational comprehension.

If liturgy is perceived as a ritual language, then the formative experience of the word of God is unleashed within the entire scope of ritual activity that pertains to this word. Children, like the rest of us, must be immersed year after year not only in the word itself, but in the entire ritual pattern of proclamation, silence, response, acclamation, homily and intercession as well as the ritual language of procession, gesture, posture, symbol and psalm. This entire ritual structure provides the formative experience of the word for children who, we hope, will gradually grow into (and not out of) the community of believers who celebrate the word of God in their lives.

This primary formative experience of the word suggests that the real issue of children at the liturgy of the word may not be their inability to understand, but rather the recurring problem of a liturgy of the word celebrated so poorly that even adults fail to understand and be formed by it.

We tolerate lectors who prepare five minutes before Mass, and lectors who may read well, but do not possess the gift of the Spirit to set out that living word magnificently and in such a way that the assembly hears this word as indeed alive and active. We incorporate music that militates against heartfelt response or acclamation: refrains that are too long, too trite, too difficult. We make poor attempts or no attempts at processions with the word. We are captive to uninspired homilists rather than captivated by good biblical preaching. We continue to build and renovate sacred spaces that do not support the word: seating designed so that most are far removed from the liturgical action and sound systems that are totally inadequate. Is it any wonder that adults, who find it difficult at best to be immersed in the word, are tempted out of genuine concern to separate the children from the assembly and provide them with something worthwhile? But even here we must be careful, as Mary Collins cautions:

> Liturgists for the young, like all of us in a consumer culture, tend to look for and to want to create novelty, not depth of experience. Ritual redundancy and repetition are not of themselves inherently boring unless they are the activities of boring people who lack both memory and imagination.[11]

What would it mean if, instead of exerting our primary energies to provide separate liturgies of the word for children on Sunday, we worked to prepare better celebrations of the word for the entire Sunday assembly— and as the *Introduction* to the Lectionary for Mass states—celebrations that are suited to all who are present?

If liturgical celebration does not look back to the founding event but renders that event present through enactment, we do a great disservice to children when we treat the readings as an historical reenactment of events in salvation history and turn the liturgy of the word into a play. Instead of proclamation we place emphasis on props, costumes, speaking parts and scenery. During particular seasons we witness the use of birthday cakes and the introduction of passion plays. Some of these activities may be appropriate for catechesis; they do not constitute liturgical celebration. Reenactment is not liturgical proclamation. Children may find it "fun" and adults may look upon it as "entertaining" or "cute," but it does not serve the nature and purpose of the liturgy of the word which interprets the word as alive and present in our midst today, taking hold of our lives within the context of contemporary human experience.

Christian Initiation of Children Who Have Reached Catechetical Age

As we have seen, the adaptation of the Rite of Christian Initiation for children of catechetical age has inaugurated a dramatic new awareness of children's capacity for responding to the word of God. The catechetical formation of these children has been accommodated to the liturgical year, rooted in the word of God and supported by celebrations of the word. The very presence of these children and their participation in the liturgical celebrations integral to the Rite have been sources of inspiration and evangelization to all in the liturgical assembly.

In light of this experience, perhaps we need to reexamine the catechetical and liturgical formation of all our children, rather than spend our resources creating separate liturgies of the word. This does not deny that young children (and all Christians!) must be enabled to grow in their understanding of the word of God, for "the more profound our understanding of the liturgical celebration, the higher our appreciation of the importance of God's word."[12] But the place for increased "understanding" is catechesis. The catechumenate for children has demonstrated that when children receive lectionary-based catechesis, when they are well nourished in the word, when the liturgical celebration of the word is integrated into their catechesis, they are enabled to participate actively and vibrantly in the liturgy of the word with the Sunday assembly.

Although relatively new, the implementation of the catechumenate for children is providing solid evidence of children's capacity for the word. Even more, we are beginning to see our own potential for developing new ways to form children in the word. Rather than the desired norm, separate liturgies of the word with children on Sundays should be celebrated rarely and only when "it is deemed appropriate."[13]

Ecclesial Relationships

Children are incorporated into the assembly by virtue of their baptism and are an integral part of its liturgical prayer because as baptized members they are in Christ. To be baptized into Christ is to enter into the prayer of Christ, to express within the liturgical assembly the worship of the living God. Since the normal Sunday assembly generally includes children, what does it mean to designate only one Mass on Sunday with a separate children's liturgy of the word? Are we mistakenly asking, "How many times a month should we prepare a special liturgy of the word for children so as to acknowledge their presence and needs?" instead of "How can we prepare the liturgy of the word in such a way as to acknowledge, welcome and embrace the presence of children who are always at our liturgies?" A fundamental aspect of Christian self-understanding—that all the baptized are brothers and sisters in Christ—is lost or effectively denied when children are excluded or ignored.

Louis Weil raises a similar question in reference to designating certain Sundays for "family eucharist" in the Episcopal Church:

> The mere presence of children does not assume an authentic family liturgy, and the evidence indicates that corporate prayer is conceived as something basically verbal and cerebral. . . . The worship of the church is the prayer-action of all its baptized members, Sunday after Sunday: children, women and men; laity and clergy. . . . Children, by their human nature and baptism, are appropriate liturgical participants even in infancy. If they are not, then it is virtually impossible to justify the church's unbroken tradition of infant baptism.[14]

Well prepared liturgies of the word that speak to all who are present, incorporate all who are present, and are suited to all who are present—these are the goal. Thus the preparation for every liturgical celebration ought to take into account the needs of children within that assembly. The *Introduction* to the Lectionary for Masses with Children, recently approved by the National Conference of Catholic Bishops, makes this statement: "The fullest reality of the liturgical assembly is children and adults together—not separate celebrations which run the risk of diminishing the place of children in the liturgical assembly."[15]

As already noted, the liturgy is the primary formative experience of church, and what we do at the liturgy affects our identity and experience of being a worshiping assembly. What are the implications of liturgical dismissals? What are we saying when we dismiss children baptized in infancy before the liturgy of the word yet dismiss unbaptized people (catechumens) after the liturgy of the word? Should we dismiss baptized children and children who are catechumens for a separate liturgy of the word, and then dismiss adult catechumens after the liturgy of the word? Do we dismiss baptized children for the liturgy of the word, reincorporate them for the liturgy of the eucharist, and then dismiss (rather than simply exclude) them from reception of the eucharist if they have not made their first communion?

In other words, the dismissal of children for a separate liturgy of the word poses fundamental questions regarding the dignity of their baptism and their relationship to the liturgical assembly. Are we, in spite of our high theology of baptism, still treating children as "pre-liturgical persons"?[16] Do our assemblies value the presence of children in their midst? Perhaps the real question is whether the Sunday assembly is ready to celebrate liturgy with children at all. As Mary Collins observes, "Adults who were not themselves disciplined by and who have not appropriated the great Christian ritual symbols and biblical stories that disclose the paschal mystery are not yet free to improvise, to create and to innovate ritually to bring children to celebration."[17]

Liturgy and Catechesis

The distinction between liturgy and catechesis is critical in this discussion because it offers a context for sorting out areas where liturgical and catechetical activities have become confused. A prime example of this confusion occurs in liturgies of the word with children when the proclamation of the word becomes a play, when lectionary readings are replaced with paraphrases of scripture, and when the homily is replaced with catechetical activity. The recent emphasis on lectionary-based catechesis has added to this confusion, unfortunately.

The liturgy of the word with children (like the liturgy of the word for all worshipers) is a ritual activity. The *Introduction* to the Lectionary for Masses with Children states:

> The church's liturgy is first and foremost ritual prayer. The liturgy of the word is neither a catechetical session nor an introduction to biblical history. The liturgy celebrates the word of God in narrative and song, makes it visible in gesture and symbol and culminates in the celebration of the eucharist.[18]

When we understand the distinction between liturgy and catechesis, we do not turn the readings into plays. We provide ministers for proclamation on the basis of liturgical competence. We strive to immerse children in the ritual pattern of the liturgy of the word rather than attempt to create innovative structures for them. We seek to ensure that the symbols, gestures and language of the liturgy of the word are similar to what the full assembly experiences. And we are careful to use music that is integral to the liturgy of the word and not substitute music that is "childish" and does not respect the ritual texts.

For these same reasons we do not use paraphrases of scripture or select without caution publications that claim to be lectionaries for children.[19] The goal of the liturgy of the word with children is the same as that for those who remain in the assembly: to hear the living and active word of God interpreting and giving meaning to their lives.

Often when children are dismissed for a separate liturgy of the word, the emphasis is on biblical instruction and not on the living word of God that leads and invites them to deeper faith. With such an emphasis, catechesis (instead of a liturgical homily) frequently follows the readings. But a homily ought to follow the proclamation of the readings, for children as well as adults. The purpose of the homily is to "lead the community of the faithful to celebrate the eucharist wholeheartedly so that they may hold fast in their lives to what they have grasped by their faith." By its very nature, the homily "should be suited to all those present, even children and the uneducated."[20] In short, "What the preacher can do best of all in this time and this place is to enable the worshiping community to celebrate by offering them a word in which they can recognize their own concerns and God's concern for them."[21]

The essence of the homily, then, is not instruction, but an invitation to prayer. It is an inherently ritual activity, based on the belief that the living word of God, proclaimed within this liturgical action, dynamically intersects with life. It is a proclamation of God's wonderful works in the history of salvation ever present and active within contemporary human experience. When we celebrate the liturgy of the word on its own terms we can see how catechesis, markedly different in purpose and method, is intimately related. Celebrations of the word that form and transform our lives lead us to seek catechesis. Catechesis enables us to reflect, interpret, articulate and internalize the faith handed on through scripture and tradition in the context of lived human experience. The deeper understanding provided in catechesis then leads us back to the worshiping assembly and deepens our experience of the liturgical celebration.

Conclusions

If the fullest expression of the liturgical assembly is children and adults at prayer together, then we have no choice but to do whatever reveals this reality. This is not to say that separate liturgies of the word for children will never be necessary; in certain situations, they may prove valuable. But the practice of children's liturgy of the word cannot become normative for the Sunday assembly.

Many other options exist for the formation for our children, options that can foster their full, active and conscious participation in the word when they are gathered with the Sunday assembly. First, we can make optimum use of adaptations for children when children comprise most of the assembly—at weekday school Masses, at religious education sessions and at sacramental preparation programs. In such instances the readings can be taken from the Lectionary for Masses with Children, the homily can be specifically prepared with their ages and abilities in mind. Ritual symbols, gestures and music that respect the nature of liturgy and the participants' capacities can be included. But even in this, we should avoid any actions or experiences that do not resemble the ritual pattern and content of the liturgy of the word as it is celebrated in the full assembly. Such experiences outside the Sunday liturgy will lead children to participate better at the Sunday liturgy of the word.

Second, we can celebrate the noneucharistic liturgies of our tradition with children—for example, reconciliation services, blessings, morning and evening prayer. We can use the occasions when children come together to pray to form them in the biblical nature of the liturgy. Instead of creating "prayer services" or praying a perfunctory opening prayer, catechists and teachers can begin and/or conclude the school day, religious education class and other catechetical session with the celebration of morning or evening prayer. Children will thus experience the ritual pattern integral to the liturgy of the word in contexts other than Mass, and at the same time they will become familiar with the psalmody of the church and our rich repertoire of liturgical symbols and gestures.

A third task is to examine the quality of catechetical formation and the role scripture plays in this formation. If liturgy is not to be confused with catechesis, then scriptural catechesis must be better integrated into religious education programs and all catechetical formation.

Fourth, sacramental catechesis must be rooted in the liturgy itself, because it is the liturgy that provides the primary source for understanding the sacrament. That is, when teaching about a particular sacrament, we should look first to the scriptural texts that are used at the celebration, to the prayers appointed for use in that liturgy, to the ritual gestures of the assembly and ministers at that liturgy. It is impossible to conceive of an adequate sacramental formation without careful attention to these various elements of the rite.

Fifth, we need a theology of childhood[22] that supports and builds on our theology of baptism. We cannot continue to treat children as "pre-liturgical" persons, or relate to children baptized in infancy as though they were catechumens. As we grow in our understanding of such a theology of childhood and its implications, the place of young children in the assembly will be clarified.

Sixth, liturgists and catechists need to work more closely together. Liturgists can help catechists better integrate liturgical dimensions into catechesis and assist in the proper preparation of liturgical celebrations. Catechists for their part can advocate the needs of young children in liturgical celebrations and provide appropriate liturgical catechesis.

Finally, we must not let poor liturgies of the word dictate liturgical and catechetical practice. Each member of the assembly—adult or child—has the right to a vibrant celebration of the liturgy of the word. Instead of separating young children from the Sunday assembly, we must work to improve the quality of the entire liturgical celebration. While this may not be easy to achieve, we look to people of vision to remind us of the goal toward which we all are striving. What does a good celebration of the liturgy of the word look like? No doubt, there are many variations and a wide range of possibilities.

In his poem "Sharon's Christmas Prayer," John Shea captures the simple and unsophisticated response of one who is captured by the marvel of God's word.

> She was five, sure of the facts, and recited them with slow solemnity, convinced
>   every word was revelation.
> She said
> they were so poor they had only peanut butter and jelly sandwiches to eat and
>   they went a long way from home without getting lost. The lady rode a
>   donkey, the man walked, and the baby was inside the lady.
> They had to stay in a stable with an ox and an ass (hee-hee) but the Three Rich
>   Men found them because a star lited the roof.
> Shepherds came and you could pet the sheep but not feed them. Then the baby
>   was borned, and do you know who he was?
> Her quarter eyes inflated
> to silver dollars.
> The baby was God.
> And she jumped in the air, whirled round, dove into the sofa, and buried her
>   head under the cushion which is the only proper response to the Good
> News of the Incarnation.[23]

Somehow the celebration of the liturgy of the word should lead all of us, each in our own way, to want to jump and whirl around because this is the only "proper response" to the proclamation of the living word of God.

Linda Gaupin

Notes

[1] Simultaneously, ritual makes a statement about the relationship between the Christian community and God as well as the community's relationship to the rest of the world.

[2] "Christian Initiation of Children Who Have Reached Catechetical Age" is the title of Part II, Chapter 1 of the *Rite of Christian Initiation of Adults* (RCIA). See the Study Edition (Chicago: Liturgy Training Publications, 1988), 155–203.

[3] Aidan Kavanagh, *On Liturgical Theology* (New York: Pueblo Publishing Co., 1984), 96–103.

[4] Editor's note: The liturgy of the word is not a dramatization of Christ with his first followers but the actual realization-in-the-doing that the same Christ is present and speaking with his followers today. On the difference between mimesis (history) and anamnesis (mystery) see among others, N. Mitchell, "The Three Days of Pascha," *Assembly* 18:1 (January 1992), 541–48; R. Taft, *Liturgy of the Hours in East and West* (Collegeville: Liturgical Press, 1986), 336–40 and "What Does Liturgy Do? Toward a Soteriology of Liturgical Celebration: Some Theses," *Worship* 66:3 (May 1992): 194–211.

[5] Aidan Kavanagh, *Confirmation: Origins and Reform* (New York: Pueblo, 1988), 31.

[6] Kavanagh, 34.

[7] Kavanagh, 17.

[8] Constance Tarasar, "'Taste and See': Orthodox Children at Worship," in Diane Apostolos-Cappadona, ed., *The Sacred Play of Children* (New York: Seabury Press, 1983), 51.

[9] Louis Weil, "Children and Worship," in Apostolos-Cappadona, ed. *The Sacred Play of Children* (New York: Seabury Press, 1983), 55.

[10] *Lectionary for Mass*, Introduction, no. 4.

[11] Mary Collins, "Is the Adult Church Ready for Liturgy with Young Christians?" in Apostolos-Cappadona, ed. *The Sacred Play of Children* (New York: Seabury Press, 1983), 15.

[12] *Lectionary for Mass*, Introduction, no. 5.

[13] *Directory for Masses with Children*, no. 19.

[14] Weil, 55.

[15] The *Lectionary for Masses with Children* will be available in September 1993. It is the only official lectionary for liturgical use with children in the United States.

[16] Weil, 15.

[17] Ibid.

[18] *Lectionary for Masses with Children*, Introduction, 13.

[19] An official lectionary for children has been a concern for many groups in the United States for the past several years. To this effect the Federation of Diocesan Liturgical Commissions approved a position statement at their National Meeting in Buffalo, New

York, in 1982, requesting that the Bishops' Committee on the Liturgy prepare a *Lectionary for Masses with Children* for use in the dioceses of the United States. See note 15 above.

[20] *Lectionary for Mass*, Introduction, no. 24.

[21] "Fulfilled in Your Hearing: The Homily in the Sunday Assembly," in *The Liturgy Documents* (Chicago: Liturgy Training Publications, 1991), 342–74; n. 14 is on p. 351–52.

[22] On the theology of childhood see K. Rahner, "Ideas for a Theology of Childhood," *Theological Investigations* 8 (1971), 33–50; N. Mitchell, "The Once and Future Child: Toward a Theology of Childhood," *Living Light* 12 (Fall 1975), 423–37; and N. Mitchell, "The Parable of Childhood," *Liturgy* 1:3 (June 1981), 7–12.

[23] John Shea, *The Hour of the Unexpected* (Allen TX: Tabor Publishing, 1977), 68.

Joan Patano Vos

Unpacking the Directory for Masses with Children

T he *Directory for Masses with Children,* issued by the Roman Congregation for Divine Worship in 1973, expresses the concern of the church at the highest level for children who have not yet entered the period of preadolescence.[1] One may wonder to what extent this serious concern has filtered down to the ordinary parish. At the parish level, the church may be as guilty as the rest of society, giving lip service to the recognition of special needs, but rarely making the changes or taking the necessary steps to serve those needs.

The *Directory for Masses with Children (Directory)* is a treasure many have yet to discover. The document should be read carefully by everyone who prepares liturgical celebrations. This "unpacking" of the *Directory* will first examine some of its "gems," statements that reveal the document's vision of the "full, conscious and authentic participation" that belongs to all by virtue of baptism and the nature of the liturgy. The practicalities of preparing and celebrating with children are considered in two parts: what is basic for all liturgical celebrations—the building blocks—and then what is important beyond those basics.

Some "Gems" of the *Directory*

The *Directory* begins on a negative but realistic note:

> Today the circumstances in which children grow up are not favorable to their spiritual progress. In addition, parents sometimes scarcely fulfill the obligations of Christian formation they accepted at the baptism of their children. . . . Although the vernacular may now be used at Mass, still the words and signs have not been sufficiently adapted to the capacity of children. . . . We may fear spiritual harm if over the years children repeatedly experience things in the church that are scarcely comprehensible to them. . . . The church follows its Master, who 'put his arms around the children . . . and blessed them' (Mark 10:16). It cannot leave children in the condition described.[2]

Let the power of this last statement ring in our ears and resound in our hearts. Since the promulgation of the *Constitution on the Sacred Liturgy* in 1963, and the publication of this *Directory* in 1973, we have stumbled liturgically in many ways, not least with regard to children.

Liturgical Formation

The centrality of the liturgy for the Christian life is highlighted at the beginning of chapter one:

> A fully Christian life cannot be conceived without participation in the liturgical services in which the faithful, gathered into a single assembly, celebrate the paschal mystery. Therefore, the religious initiation of children must be in harmony with this purpose. . . . It is not right to separate the liturgical and eucharistic formation from the general human and Christian education of children. Indeed it would be harmful if liturgical formation lacked such a foundation.[3]

This statement also presumes that initiation is a continual process rooted in human experience. We have begun to retrieve this understanding, especially since the restoration of the catechumenate for adults and children of catechetical age.

There are human values found in eucharistic celebrations that are essential to Christian formation: "activity of the community, exchange of greetings, capacity to listen and to seek and grant pardon, expression of gratitude, experience of symbolic actions, a meal of friendship, and festive celebration."[4] Mark Searle expresses this conviction in *Liturgy Made Simple:*

> It [the liturgy] teaches us to use our bodies to house the presence of God, to worship him and to serve him, and to bring his word and healing to others. It teaches us to listen to the voice of God in the voice of others, and to receive at the hands of others the gifts of God. It teaches us to live in the society of others, people of different background and different race, as men and women committed to peace and unity and mutual help. It teaches us to use the goods of the earth—represented in the liturgy by bread and wine and water and oil—not as goods to be grabbed, accumulated and consumed, but as sacraments of the Creator, to be accepted with thanksgiving, handled with reverence and shared with generosity.[5]

The indispensable role of parents in Christian formation—mentioned already in the first article of the *Directory*—is examined more thoroughly in article ten. Parents teach their children how to pray by praying with them, teaching them family prayers and bringing them "even from their early years" to join gradually in the prayer of the church. This is the age-old understanding that there is no greater teacher than example. "The Christian family has the greatest role in instilling these Christian and human values. Thus Christian education, provided by parents and other educators, should be strongly encouraged in relation to the liturgical formation of children as well." The three vital elements, then, are the family, religious education programs and the liturgy. Together they form a unity, each providing an essential component in the Christian formation of a child.

But this does not free the rest of the community from its responsibility. The witness of the entire parish is essential in the formation of Christians:

> The Christian communities to which the individual families belong or in which the children live also have a responsibility toward children baptized in the church. By giving witness to the gospel, living familial charity, and actively celebrating the mysteries of Christ, the Christian community is the best school of Christian and liturgical formation for the children who live in it.[6]

If our children do not see a community striving to live the gospel, formal religious education will not do much good. All of us, particularly the members of the community who do not have children or whose children are grown and no longer at home, need to be reminded of the formative power our own Christian witness has on the young people of our communities.

A related statement from article 16—"the witness of adult believers can have a great effect upon the children"—brings to mind all those times that as a child I attended Mass with my mother. I remember that she almost always cried at the time of the consecration. I did not understand why, but I knew that something powerful was happening. Perhaps her strong witness revealed to me in unconscious ways that all of life's sufferings and joys welled up and burst forth in the presence of the divine.

But as article 16 is quick to add, this witnessing is a two-way street for Christians: "Adults can in turn benefit spiritually from experiencing the part that children have within the Christian community." How many members of any given community are able to recognize or admit the spiritual benefit they gain from the presence of children at the liturgy? We often forget that "in their own way children are genuinely capable of reflection."[7] The role of adults in the church is not to "put God into children." Rather, we help to shape an environment where they feel at home in and with the divine presence. And then we need to pray with them.

The Whole Body at Prayer

Worship is an activity of the whole person and of the whole church, the Body of Christ. Everyone is to participate with "heart and mind, soul and body" and each person is to do his or her part. Both principles must be kept in mind lest "the liturgy . . . appear as something dry and merely intellectual"[8] or fail to express the wondrous diversity of ministries that flow from the gifts of the Spirit.

Article 33 states explicitly: "The development of gestures, postures and actions is very important . . . in view of the nature of the liturgy as an activity of the entire person." We do not have to invent new gestures, but we can certainly make better use of the gestures and postures of our tradition: the sign of the cross, genuflection or bow, kneeling, sitting, standing, carrying things reverently and so on. We could remember to include children in the various processions—at the gathering, with the book of the gospels, at the preparation of the gifts, as well as in the communion procession.

Bodily actions are not the whole of participation, however. "External activities will be fruitless and even harmful if they do not serve the internal participation of the children. Thus, religious silence has its importance even in Masses with children."[9] Silence is perhaps the most neglected element of the renewed liturgy.

The *Directory* includes other principles that can help to ensure full, conscious and active participation. Article 25 speaks of a space suited to the number of participants: "It should be a place where the children can act with a feeling of ease according to the requirements of a living liturgy that is suited to their age." Article 26 suggests sensitivity to the time of day that Mass is celebrated; the time should correspond to the circumstances of their lives and the daily cycle of their energies. And article 28 suggests that the group celebrating Mass together not be too large, but that instead the students be divided into smaller groups, "with regard for the children's progress in religious formation and catechetical preparation."

Ministries

Article 22 encourages the full diversity of ministries that are the norm for every Sunday Mass. Children (and adults!) are meant to participate in every way possible according to their gifts. Sharing the gift that the Spirit has given to each one for the sake of "building up the body" is the essence of all Christian ministry, liturgical and otherwise. The diversity of ministries is the strongest evidence that the Mass is not a celebration belonging to a single minister but to a community with a variety of gifts.[10]

On Sundays and feast days, when they celebrate with the rest of the community, the children may be given some tasks within the liturgy such as singing parts of the Mass. This language can be ambiguous unless we remember that any activity taken on by members of the assembly is done for the good of the whole community's prayer, not simply to give somebody something to do. Nor should the children (or the adults) be given liturgical tasks or functions unless they are so gifted, rehearsed and prepared.

Role of the Presider

The *Directory* recognizes that a priest may "find it difficult to adapt himself to the mentality of the children," i.e, not all priest-presiders have the necessary gifts for preaching well when many children are in the assembly.

One of the adults who is so gifted may speak to the children after the gospel.[13] It is also possible on occasion for the children to share their own insights in a dialog homily.[14] We may take these guidelines for granted today, but in 1973 they were innovations!

There is no denying that the *Directory* places rather heavy demands on the presider. They are not unreasonable demands but should be understood as long-term goals or ideals that can help improve one's presidential and ministerial style all across the board:

> It is the responsibility of the priest who celebrates with children to make the celebration festive, familial and meditative. Even more than in Masses with adults, the priest is the one to create this kind of attitude, which depends on his personal preparation and his manner of acting and speaking with others. The priest should be concerned above all about the dignity, clarity and simplicity of his actions and gestures. In speaking to the children he should express himself so that he will be easily understood, while avoiding any childish style of speech.[15]

Some priests have a natural manner of acting and speaking that is particularly attractive to children. But others can achieve the attitude and style called for if they are willing to engage in careful preparation and studied evaluation of their presidential styles on a regular basis. Both the preparation and the evaluation should be done in conversation with the teachers of the school, and perhaps some of the students, if presiders hope to gain an accurate view of the needs they will be serving. This work makes one vulnerable, yet isn't spiritual vulnerability part of the gift that children bring to us? If the presider does not develop a rapport with children outside the liturgy, no amount of preparation or rehearsal will enable him to "connect" with the children inside the liturgy and effectively lead them in prayer.[16]

Frequency of Masses

Paradoxically, one major obstacle to full participation may be the frequency of the celebrations:

> Weekday Mass in which children participate can certainly be celebrated with greater effect and less danger of boredom, if it does not take place every day. Moreover, preparation can be more careful if there is a longer interval between diverse celebrations.[17]

This guideline should be first in any examination of school liturgical practices. If the celebrations are too frequent for there to be careful planning on the part of the children and adults involved, then the first change to begin discussing with the leaders—pastor, liturgist, principal, teachers—is reducing the number of Masses.[12]

Adapting the Roman Rite for Children

"From the beginning of the liturgical reform it has been clear to everyone that some adaptations are necessary in these Masses [with children in which only a few adults participate]."[17] This statement must be read in conjunction with the section on cultural adaptation from the *Constitution on the Sacred Liturgy* (37–40). Adaptations, the *Constitution* insists, are permitted and even encouraged, "provided that the substantial unity of the Roman Rite is preserved." Most adaptations are made at the level of the national conference of bishops; others are necessary for individual celebrations. We who work with children and the liturgy should understand the Mass of the Roman Rite sufficiently to preserve its integrity.

For example, caution is recommended before implementing article 22 of the *Directory*—"To encourage participation, it will sometimes be helpful to have several additions, for example, the insertion of motives for giving thanks before the priest begins the dialogue of the preface." When participants are properly prepared and when Mass is celebrated well, its rhythm and shape are fairly apparent and there is little need for additions. Thus, before we can even think about changing or upsetting the balance of the rite, we need to help students and adults alike experience and understand that rhythm and shape. We learn by celebrating the liturgy carefully and consistently year after year. Our work is not to change or add as much as it is to submit to the rite, to experience the mystery it reveals, and to explore the layers of meaning so that we *and* the children can experience a deeper and fuller encounter with our Creator God through Jesus Christ.

The very purpose of the *Directory* is to guide our choices and our preparations so that the adaptations are not deformations of the liturgy. We must remember that the liturgy belongs to the whole church.

The Basics

Begin with Lectionary and Sacramentary, Feast and Season

In order to prepare any liturgy, one must know how to locate the liturgy for the day: the solemnity, feast, memorial or weekday that is celebrated, the readings and prayers that are assigned, the songs that are suggested. Every parish and school should have an ordo or an official church calendar (these are published each year). The ordo indicates what liturgy is to be celebrated, which texts are assigned, which aspects of the liturgy are required and which are optional. The most important liturgical books are the lectionary, which includes readings for every day of the year and for many special occasions, and the sacramentary, which contains all the texts and prayers for the presider as well as suggested antiphons for the entrance and communion processions.

Along with the assigned readings and prayers, the liturgical season shapes our celebrations. The children need to know and talk about the spirit of each season. We can help them understand gradually that Advent is a time of anticipating the birth of a new creation and the many "comings" of the Messiah, not only a time of waiting for the birth of a baby. Christmas is a celebration of the Word-made-flesh, the wedding of divinity and humanity, not just a birthday party for Jesus. Lent is a time of preparation for renewing our baptism. Easter celebrates not only Jesus' resurrection, but his and our passion and death and resurrection and hope and mission. Ordinary Time doesn't mean "the same old boring stuff"! It is a time to break open our ordinary lives to see the divine presence dwelling and revealed within.

Music

Although the *Directory* does not comment much on music, the United States bishops' document, *Music in Catholic Worship*[18] does provide essential guidelines. All the musical elements of the Mass are described and prioritized so that music will always support and serve the rite.

Music in Catholic Worship gives highest priority to the singing of the acclamations: the alleluia, the acclamations during the eucharistic prayer, and the doxology to the Lord's Prayer.[19] Everyone should know the musical settings for these acclamations by heart!

Next in importance are the processional songs at the entrance and communion.[20] The functions of the gathering song are to gather us into one community, accompany the entrance procession and reflect the season. This music is often a hymn but can be a song with a refrain or even a litany. The communion song should foster a sense of unity and support the ritual action of gathering around the table to share in communion. A hymn that requires participants to hold a book distracts from the procession and inhibits the reception of communion. Thus the communion song should consist of either a communal refrain with the choir or cantor singing the verses, or an ostinato (a short refrain in the style of a mantra) as is found in the music of Taizé.

With regard to the actual songs and settings that are chosen, "It is always necessary to keep in mind that these eucharistic celebrations (Masses with children in which only a few adults participate) must lead children toward the celebration of Mass with adults, especially the Masses at which the Christian community must come together on Sundays."[21] In other words, we should be using the same repertoire with children on weekdays that we use at the Sunday liturgy. The songs we teach our children for worship should last them a lifetime and be worthy of passing on to their children and grandchildren.

At the level of the "basics," then, the music required for every liturgy includes the gathering song, the acclamations as outlined above and the communion song. It is wonderful when the students know this music so well that it simply pours forth from within them. Once they have mastered this much they can begin to add other hymns and songs.

Liturgy of the Word

A brief comment on the scripture translations used for Masses with children: Children do not have to comprehend every detail of the liturgical experience. We may actually do the children a disservice if, within the context of the liturgy, we use translations like the *Good News Bible* or some other personal modification or simplification of the text instead of the same translation used in the Sunday assembly. Over the years, as we grow in age and wisdom, our ears are trained or tuned to the sounds of the words in scripture verses. They are like good pieces of music. We learn them early on and then their beauty and message live with us and grow with us, calling forth from us an ever deeper spiritual response. We have a responsibility to pass on to our children the very shapes and sounds of words that we hear proclaimed in the liturgy so they can grow into them. Translations or modifications may be useful in the children's telling and retelling of the stories before and after the liturgy. But the word proclaimed should be the same pattern of words that we all know and share together at prayer.

The general intercessions conclude the liturgy of the word and give voice to the needs that rise in our hearts as we reflect on the readings and on how, where or with whom this part of God's story is not being fulfilled. These intentions are to be general and inclusive even when specific people are mentioned.[22] We always pray for the needs of the church, the world, those with special needs, our community, this assembly, the deceased.

The chosen reader(s) should have the petitions a few days in advance to rehearse not only reading, but praying these words from the heart. If a group of students is going to read them, they should be in place when the intercessions begin, well-rehearsed in the sequence and rhythm of the prayers. They should stand still until after the presider has completed the concluding prayer.

Liturgy of the Eucharist

The preparation of the gifts calls for a procession with real bread and wine. If, in the course of their liturgical catechesis, children could experience the sowing, sprouting, harvesting and grinding of the wheat, and the kneading, mixing and baking of the dough that provides the bread for the eucharist and also be exposed to the process by which wine is made from grapes, then the use of a single loaf of unleavened bread and a worthy decanter of wine will provide an immediate entryway into the mystery of the eucharist that no amount of explanation could ever supply. The *way* in which the bread and wine are carried up the aisle, presented to the presider and placed on the altar helps to reveal their symbolic meaning and prepares the assembly to experience them as the bread of life and the cup of salvation when they are transformed in prayer and received in communion.

The central prayer of the liturgy, the eucharistic prayer, is sometimes experienced as the most uninteresting. This does not have to be the case if we note carefully what the *Directory* says in its regard:

> The eucharistic prayer is of the greatest importance in the eucharist celebrated with children because it is the high point of the entire celebration. Much depends upon the manner in which the priest proclaims this prayer and in which the children take part by listening and making their acclamations.[23]

Again, it is the *way* the prayer is proclaimed and the *way* the children listen and acclaim. Listening is a valuable skill and a vital form of participation in communal prayer. The temptation is to neglect listening and concentrate solely on the acclamations. Catechesis for liturgy should include not only rehearsal of the eucharistic acclamations, but practice in imaginative listening.

At the same time, the presider's role in this prayer is of paramount importance:

> The disposition of mind required for this central part of the celebration, the calm and reverence with which everything is done, should make the children as attentive as possible.[24]

If the presider remembers that this is a prayer addressed to God through Christ in the Holy Spirit and not a play of the Last Supper with a monologue addressed to the assembly, the children will know they are listening to someone *speak to God* and be led naturally into the praying of this thanksgiving. If all the adults present show by their own body language the proper way to participate in this prayer, the children will know by intuition that this is a special moment in the celebration. Then, the sung acclamations that they *know by heart* will truly come *from the heart*.

Since the *Directory* first appeared, three eucharistic prayers for Masses with children have been approved. They include more frequent acclamations than the other eucharistic prayers, and their vocabulary and images were chosen especially with children in mind. These prayers, found at the back of the sacramentary, are a good choice when celebrating with children.

Communion under both forms is part of "the basics" in Masses with children, as it is in Masses with any assembly. The bread and the wine together are the sacrifice and the meal. The cup is not reserved for adults. Special Masses with children are good occasions to accustom children to sharing in the cup.

Preparing the Liturgy Means Preparing Ourselves

Every member of the assembly needs to prepare for the liturgy. Although some have specific roles that require additional training and rehearsal, all can benefit from what is most basic—reflection on the readings.[25] This does not necessarily mean theological analysis or exegesis of the assigned scriptures. It does mean entering the world of the text, participating in the questions posed and in the conversations and actions described, and finding in this "myth"[26] the expression of our own life story.

For example, adults can spend time with children, reading the passage, letting them retell the story in their own words, then allowing them to make connections in their own lives or simply to be familiar with the passage. They can be free to talk, act, draw, sing about it at their own level of reflection. They do not need you to give them "the message" of the readings, but to allow them to respond to the narrative, prophecy or instruction at their own level of experience, and to encourage their discussion.

The *Directory* calls for word services in order to provide the children with more exposure to the scriptures.[27] Short, simple prayer services that use the scripture texts for next Sunday's liturgy can help prepare children for the experience of that word as it will be proclaimed in the Mass. Care should be taken that such word services do not have the tone of a classroom exercise.

Liturgy is a ritual celebration that can only be set free by familiarity. We cannot expect children (or adults) to have an authentic, liberating experience in the liturgy if they are not familiar with the word. Brief scripture services permit the word to come to life within us and among us. When the students begin spontaneously to quote or allude to the scriptures within the context of other lessons, or scriptural images begin appearing in their conversation or artwork, then you know the scriptures are taking root in their hearts and imaginations.[28]

Preparing ourselves for the liturgy of the eucharist can take several forms. We can practice the sung acclamations of the eucharistic prayer. The text of the prayer itself can be used as an activity or discussion starter—e.g., "Look at all the things we praise God for!" Or, "Look at how Jesus cared for people who needed him." Or, "Listen for all the things we ask God for." We can open up the symbols of bread and wine with the children, and connect our sharing at God's table with other meals we share. We can practice the communion procession, going over how we walk, sing, hold our hands, receive the bread and the cup, return to our places. When these activities are done in an atmosphere of joy, children and adults can internalize the patterns and thus come more prepared to celebrate the liturgy.

Rehearsing the Ministers

Every school could consider establishing a ministry training program for students, similar and related to the program for preparing ministers for the Sunday assembly. Those students who exhibit a particular gift for proclamation could form a pool to serve as lectors on a rotating basis and perhaps become a part of the Sunday rotation.[29] The same could be done for all student liturgical ministries. This is a more authentic approach to liturgical ministry than simply choosing a different student each time. Identification with a certain role provides a sense of belonging and purpose. It can heighten the liturgical experience and provide students with goals and opportunities to place their gifts at the service of the entire community.

Although some ministries require more training or skill, every liturgical role should be spoken of and treated as equal in importance to the others. Each student should be called upon to do well what he or she can do, to see the dignity and holiness of this service, and to strive to do it prayerfully. This includes the role of the assembly. In small group Masses the assembly's role can be especially emphasized because it is easier to see one another and to be influenced by the enthusiastic participation of others.

In addition to participating as members in the assembly, children may serve as readers, singers in the choir, cantors, gift bearers, altar servers (to carry cross, candle, incense), book bearers. Each of these ministries requires some training and rehearsal.[30]

The one who carries the book of the gospels, for example, carries a holy object. How should she hold the book? How should she walk in procession? Rehearsals ought to include not only the externals, but the underlying attitude, "the internal participation," in the words of article 22.

Liturgy Includes More Than Words

A good example of the importance of nonverbal elements in liturgy is the procession. A liturgical procession is not an ordinary walk, nor is it a parade or a foot race. Every procession should convey an awareness of Christ present in and through the assembly. As such, it is prayer. All who are involved—cross bearer, candle bearers, a book bearer, eucharistic ministers, even the whole assembly[31]—could rehearse the gathering procession. The students who bring the bread and the wine to the altar need to practice so that the primary focus of attention is on the gifts and the ritual movement of the assembly from the table of the word to the table of the eucharist. Although the children may find it humorous at first to rehearse ritual actions, their attitude will be shaped in large part by the reverent enthusiasm of the adults assisting them.

Silence, too, is prayer. The *Directory* reminds us that silence is an integral part of the worship experience,[32] but in a culture that abhors silence, children and adults alike may need help to understand how to use these moments of corporate silence for prayer, meditation and reflection. Praying in silence is a skill that can be rehearsed and learned.

One nonverbal prayer the *Directory* does not mention is the sign of peace. This gesture, like sharing in communion, is a public act that reveals a commitment to be like Christ in all that we do. It shows our willingness to do whatever we must in order to be reconciled, in order to allow Christ's peace to penetrate our world. Practicing this gesture with children and talking about its meaning could help prepare them for a fuller experience of this moment of the Mass.

The arrangement and decoration of the space are visual elements of the prayer. Unfortunately, "decorating" often takes more time, energy and resources than all the other preparations put together. At the level of the basics, we need to ensure that the objects, vessels and books are of the best quality and condition available. Loose leaf sheets and missalettes are inappropriate in the sanctuary.[33] Lectors should read from the lectionary. Intercessions can be placed in a three-ring binder covered in fabric and coordinated with the color of the liturgical season.[34]

Beyond the Basics

After the basics have been mastered—no small accomplishment—it is possible to move beyond them to strengthen other aspects of the liturgy.

Joan Patano Vos

Liturgy of the Word

The *Directory* suggests "when the text of the readings lends itself to this, it may be helpful to have the children read it with parts distributed among them, as is provided for the reading of the Lord's passion during Holy Week."[35] But this is not the same thing as turning the "reading" of scripture into a play. Props and costumes belong in a theater! Stories or certain poetic texts may or may not take well to this division into parts.

A brief introduction to the readings is mentioned in article 47 of the *Directory* and in article 11 of the *General Instruction of the Roman Missal.* But before preparing such a commentary, keep in mind that if the students have spent time preparing for the liturgy by reflecting together on the scriptures, commentary is unnecessary and can even work to the detriment of the celebration by turning it into a didactic experience.

Singing the responsorial psalm will enable a fuller experience of the scriptures and provide another opportunity for music. Students with musical ability can be trained in the role of cantor and song leader. This can become a part of the student ministry training program.

Another area for strengthening the ritual action is the gospel procession. Such processions are not common practice, even on feasts, in the average parish. Yet this procession offers ways to involve children, especially through the use of candles and graceful gestures. The procession helps to focus the assembly's attention on the gospel proclamation as the high point of the liturgy of the word.

Liturgy of the Eucharist

The procession with bread and wine ritualizes in representative form what originally consisted of a procession with gifts for the poor carried out by the entire assembly. There are occasions when this fuller form of the procession will be appropriate and beneficial.[36] Everyone could bring nonperishables, clothing or money with them to their places in the church, and present these along with the bread and wine during the procession. These gifts could be placed in specially decorated boxes or baskets, and the children themselves could accompany those who deliver the gifts to the poor.

As the children develop their listening skills, their acclamations can be enhanced by the playing of musical instruments and the use of prayerful gestures. It is not necessary that these gestures "mime" the words of the acclamations or of the eucharistic prayer itself. Instead, the children can raise their hands in prayer, bow their heads or bow from the waist, and even clap their hands if a musical setting so demands. The postures, gestures and movements should enhance and deepen the experience of the prayer without replacing the prayer or getting in the way.

Music

Once the processional songs, acclamations, and responsorial psalm are being sung well, the litanies (Lord, have mercy and Lamb of God) can be added, with a cantor or choir leading them. The Glory to God should be sung on feasts as assigned in the ordo, especially the feast of the patron saint. The Lord's Prayer can be sung, and the general intercessions always flow better when a cantor sings the intentions and the assembly sings its response.

These musical elements should not be added arbitrarily, but should reflect the rank of the feast or season. Days with the rank of "Solemnity" or "Feast" should be celebrated with as much singing as possible. Students who play musical instruments can enhance and support the singing or play an instrumental piece during the preparation of the gifts on special occasions.[37] On ordinary weekdays, the basic music is sufficient. When using music at the secondary musical moments, the actual song must not create an imbalance that overwhelms the more important and basic musical moments.

A list of acclamations, responses, hymns and songs that the students know and sing enthusiastically will save time and energy in making choices and free the children to sing "from the heart" what they know by heart. Planners or teachers may be tempted to choose what is different or new, without attention to how well the children are singing. Variety may be the spice of life, but excessive variety is the death of ritual prayer.

When planning music, we should be careful to choose the musical form that is best suited to a particular part of the rite. Hymns such as "Praise to the Lord" work best when all or most are standing still. Songs with refrains and verses, such as "Now We Remain" or any responsorial psalm, work well for processions in which many of the assembly participate. Ostinatos, such as "Jesus, Remember Me," can also work well for processions.

The Environment

Art used as a means to explore or express a scripture passage or the liturgical season should probably remain in the classroom. A long term project, over a period of months and used in a final school liturgy, with the participation of all of the students in the school—a carefully crafted collage, hanging, or fabric art made into a vestment, altar or ambo hanging—would more readily reflect the quality and effort that the liturgy deserves. Such a piece should be worthy of use at the Sunday liturgy; it could be a gift from the students to the rest of the parish.

There are unlimited possibilities for other kinds of artistic work that can enhance the liturgy; for example, children can fashion banners that add festivity to processions. However, this work should be directed by someone who has a keen understanding of liturgical principles, the rhythm of the ritual and the nature of art.

Conclusion

To prepare the basics and celebrate the liturgy well is a challenge that can keep us and the children busy for a lifetime. A perfect celebration is not one in which everything goes as planned (such a liturgy exists only in heaven) but one in which the participants have known God's gift of self to us and made Christ's prayer of thanks and praise their own. This is no easy task, but the work is not ours alone. I am always comforted by the wisdom of Mother Teresa of Calcutta: We are not called to be successful, only faithful—faithful to the gospel, to our ancient and living tradition, and to our children.

Notes

1. *Directory for Masses with Children* (DMC), no. 6. The DMC is published in the introductory material of the sacramentary. It is included in *The Liturgy Documents*, third edition, (Chicago: Liturgy Training Publications, 1991), 235–47.

[2] DMC, nos. 1–3.

[3] DMC, no. 8.

[4] DMC, no. 9.

[5] *Liturgy Made Simple* (Collegeville: Liturgical Press, 1981), 27.

[6] DMC, no. 11.

[7] DMC, no. 37.

[8] DMC, no. 35.

[9] DMC, no. 22.

[10] See DMC, no. 24, and the *Constitution on the Sacred Liturgy,* no. 28.

[11] DMC, no. 27.

[12] In scheduling Masses for the school year, feasts and seasons should be the framework. Consult the *Leader's Manual: Hymnal for Catholic Students* (Chicago: Liturgy Training Publications, 1989) for more background.

[13] DMC, no. 24.

[14] DMC, no. 48.

[15] DMC, no. 23.

[16] Choosing the presidential prayers may be another opportunity for involving and preparing and catechizing the children. This also gives the children and presider an occasion to meet outside the liturgy.

[17] DMC, no. 20.

[18] *Music in Catholic Worship* (MCW), Bishops' Committee on the Liturgy, 1972 (revised edition, 1982); see also *Liturgical Music Today* (1982). Both are found in *The Liturgy Documents.*

[19] MCW, nos. 53–54. See also DMC, no. 30.

[20] MCW, nos. 60–62.

[21] DMC, no. 21.

[22] For example, "For all the sick, especially Tommy Smith and Margaret Johnson's grandmother, let us pray to the Lord."

[23] DMC, no. 52.

[24] Ibid.

[25] DMC, nos. 41–47.

[26] Joseph Campbell's study of the myths of various cultures provides a way of rediscovering scripture as story. He has shown that myths are powerful stories in which the mysteries of

life, death and resurrection are spoken. *Joseph Campbell and the Power of Myth,* Video recording in 6 parts: *The Hero's Adventure, The Message of the Myth, Sacrifice and Bliss, Love and the Goddess, The First Storytellers, Masks of Eternity* (New York: Mystic Fire Video, 1988).

[27] DMC, nos. 13–14.

[28] See Paul Philibert's article beginning on page 10 of this volume.

[29] *A Well-Trained Tongue* (Chicago: Liturgy Training Publications, 1982) is an excellent resource for preparing lectors—students and adults alike.

[30] See DMC, no. 22.

[31] See DMC, no. 34.

[32] DMC, nos. 22, 37.

[33] Missalettes are temporary aids, thrown away each month or season, and are not printed on quality material. Students would have little reason to treat them with respect.

[34] Perhaps these covers could be a project for children in the upper grades.

[35] DMC, no. 47.

[36] The sacramentary permits this kind of procession and strongly recommends it for the Evening Mass of the Lord's Supper on Holy Thursday.

[37] DMC, no. 32.

Editors and Contributors

Eleanor Bernstein, CSJ, is director of the Center for Pastoral Liturgy. She brings a wide background in education and pastoral liturgy to the planning and coordination of the Center's workshops and conferences. She has served as coeditor of *Assembly* and written for several pastoral liturgical publications.

John Brooks-Leonard served as associate director for education at the Notre Dame Center for Pastoral Liturgy and had the primary responsibility for the design and coordination of the Twentieth Annual Conference, "Children of Promise: A Place in the Assembly." He is the author of *Leading the Community in Prayer* (a videotape on presiding) and many articles on liturgical topics.

Linda Gaupin, CDP, is associate director of the Secretariat of the Bishops' Committee on the Liturgy and works with the Consultations on Children of the North American Forum on the Catechumenate. Her essay "Let Those Who Have Faith Not Be Hasty: Penance and Children," appears in *Reconciliation: The Continuing Agenda,* Robert J. Kennedy, editor.

Gertrud Mueller Nelson is a speaker, author and artist in Del Mar, California. Her background includes work in Montessori education and Jungian psychology. *To Dance with God* is a further exposition of ideas presented in her essay in this volume.

Paul Philibert, OP, is provincial superior of the Dominican Friars in the southern United States, New Orleans, Louisiana. He is a writer and speaker, and served on the faculty of The Catholic University of America, where he was director of the Center for the Study of Youth Development.

Mark Searle was associate professor of theology at the University of Notre Dame, former associate director of the Notre Dame Center for Pastoral

Liturgy and editor of *Assembly.* He published numerous articles and books on the theology of the liturgy and the pastoral implementation of the liturgical reform. *Christening: The Making of Christians* focuses on the history and theology of the rites of Christian initiation. Mark Searle died on August 16, 1992.

Joan Patano Vos is a lecturer and author residing in Woodland Hills, California. She previously served as the director of the Office of Worship in Wichita, as a parish musician and liturgist, and as a classroom teacher. Her book *Celebrating School Liturgies* is a pastoral guide to implementing the *Directory for Masses with Children.*